Legends of Texas Barbecue Cookbook

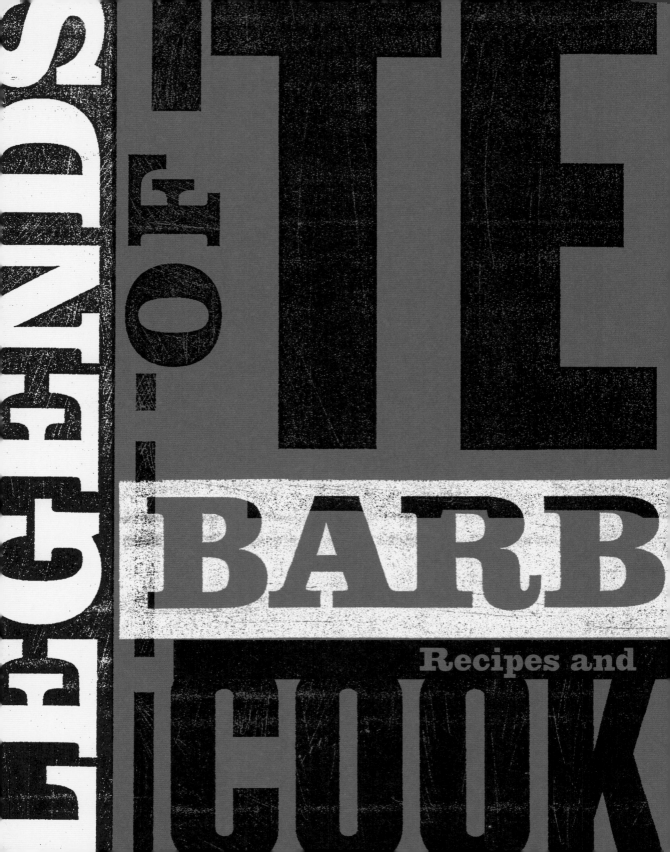

TEXAS BARBECUE

ROBB WALSH

FOREWORD BY JEFFREY W. SAVELL

ECUE

Recollections from the Pitmasters

CHRONICLE BOOKS
SAN FRANCISCO

pages 2–3: Captain Will Wright of the Texas Rangers cooks his dinner over a campfire (circa 1930).
Photo: Texas State Library Archives Division

pages 4–5: A barbecue stand made of corrugated tin, Corpus Christi, 1939.
Photo by Russell Lee

Library of Congress Cataloging-in-Publication Data available.
ISBN 978-1-4521-3998-2

Manufactured in China

Designed by Erin Mayes and DJ Stout, Pentagram, Austin
Typesetting by River Jukes-Hudson
Diagrams by A.J. Garces, with revisions on page 241 by Amanda Fung

10 9 8 7 6 5 4 3 2 1

Chronicle Books LLC
680 Second Street
San Francisco, California 94107
www.chroniclebooks.com

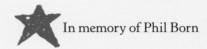 In memory of Phil Born

Mopping the meat at the Annual
Millheim Father's Day Barbecue

A far-flung family dynasty—each of the four Mikeska brothers built a barbecue restaurant in a different Texas town. Left to right: Jerry, Maurice, Rudy (deceased), and Clem.
Photo by Will van Overbeek

Dr. Savell at Barbecue Summer Camp.

Foreword

My first encounter with *Legends of Texas Barbecue Cookbook* by Robb Walsh occurred one summer day about ten years ago in a Harry & David's store in San Marcos, Texas. While my wife was shopping, I happened on a display featuring the book. I picked one up and began to browse through it. Impressed by the blend of history and recipes, I somewhat absentmindedly carried it with me to the checkout counter and added it to my wife's pile of merchandise. Now, looking back on that day, it's amazing what a profound impact that impulse purchase had on how I have spent the last six years of my life.

I read the book when we got home and then put it on our cookbook shelf, ready to pick up again when a good barbecue recipe was needed. But *Legends of Texas Barbecue* would end up playing a far greater role in my life than that.

In the spring of 2009, Texas A&M University asked the faculty to teach first-year seminars for incoming freshmen. These one-hour courses for small groups would feature subjects the students might find interesting, but the real goal was to give ten to fifteen freshmen contact with professors who could help them make the transition from high school to college.

The pilot program in 2008 included a class on baseball taught by a history professor. As a meat science professor, I immediately thought, if you can teach a course on baseball, why not a course on Texas barbecue? And I knew that I already had the perfect textbook for the class: Robb Walsh's *Legends of Texas Barbecue Cookbook*.

Texas Barbecue, now known as ANSC 117 in the Texas A&M course catalog, was first taught in the fall of 2009. During the semester, I got an e-mail from none other than Robb Walsh seeking assistance with a story he was working on about fajitas. I told him I recognized his name because I was using his book for the barbecue class. Instead of answering his questions about the meat cuts used for fajitas, I invited him to come and visit the Meat Science Center for a hands-on demonstration of the various cuts.

When Robb showed up on campus, I asked him to come back and talk to the class. And he has come back every year since that first visit. The twenty-five lucky freshmen who take the course get to hear one of the most knowledgeable guest lecturers on barbecue around, and they also get Robb Walsh to personally autograph their textbooks.

If the story ended there, it would be great, but there is more. In May 2010, I invited Robb to the Texas A&M Beef Center to participate in Beef 101, our three-day course on learning everything about beef, from the live animal to the final products. I also invited him to be a guest speaker at the university's Rosenthal Lecture Series, to bring our students up-to-date on popular topics affecting the meat industry, such as nose-to-tail cookery.

Whenever we talked, Robb told me about his dream of creating an organization to preserve our food culture in Texas, much as the University of Mississippi–based Southern Foodways Alliance does for the South. I told Robb that Texas A&M would be glad to help, but that the Department of Animal Science did not do cultural and historical documentation—that we are, after all, agricultural subject-matter experts.

Despite my protestations, in July 2010, Robb talked me into providing the lecture hall at the Beef Center as a venue for the all-day meeting of fifty key leaders in the Texas food scene. That gathering gave birth to Foodways Texas, whose mission is to preserve, promote, and celebrate the diverse food cultures of Texas. The organization is now head-quartered at the University of Texas at Austin. Somehow, I ended up sitting on its first board of directors.

To be successful, Foodways Texas needed to conduct educational programs that appealed to the public. The Texas barbecue scene was undergoing a renaissance at the time, fueled by coverage from television shows and the rapid response that social media created whenever someone discovered a great new barbecue joint.

Robb and I brainstormed a barbecue seminar and a hands-on workshop that combined food culture and food science, with catering provided by star pitmasters. The logical place to hold it was the Texas A&M Meat Science Center, where we would have meat cutting labs and sides of beef and whole hogs at our disposal—not to mention a bunch of meat science professors and graduate students who were passionate about barbecue.

The first Barbecue Summer Camp, a joint venture between Foodways Texas and Texas A&M University, was held in June 2011. We thought it would appeal to backyard barbecue enthusiasts, but we were humbled by the number of cook-off winners, master chefs, and other experts who showed up.

Enthusiastic press coverage, blog write-ups, and just plain word of mouth resulted in sellouts every time the seminar has been held. To satisfy the demand for barbecue instruction, we started Camp Brisket in January 2013, which, as the name implies, focuses on this most difficult of all cuts. Tickets for Camp Brisket 2015 sold out in two minutes.

Thanks to the give and take between instructors and some of the most knowledgeable students of barbecue imaginable, Barbecue Summer Camp and Camp Brisket are keeping on top of changes in Texas barbecue and providing help in understanding new techniques, new equipment, and newly popular cuts of meat. In this second edition of *Legends of Texas Barbecue Cookbook*, Robb Walsh has covered much of this new information—a task made easier by his vantage point from a front-row seat at every Barbecue Summer Camp held to date.

Robb is my favorite food writer because of the way his stories about the culture and history of foods breathe life into the recipes he details. Few writers have this magic. Enjoy the journey that this new edition continues, take pleasure in the stories, and gain the cooking insights you need to tackle each recipe with the confidence of a veteran pitmaster!

JEFFREY W. SAVELL

University Distinguished Professor,
Leader, Meat Science Section,
Department of Animal Science,
Texas A&M University

Introduction

TEXANS BARBECUE BEEF.

THESE THREE WORDS ARE OFTEN USED TO SUM UP THE TEXAS barbecue experience. I understand why this knee-jerk explanation has become so popular; it reduces a long, complicated saga into a pat one-liner that no one can really disagree with. The real story of Texas barbecue is far more bewildering.

Southern barbecue is a proud thoroughbred whose bloodlines are easily traced. Texas barbecue is a feisty mutt with a whole lot of crazy relatives. The Southern barbecue style has remained largely unchanged over time. Texas barbecue is constantly evolving.

Before the Civil War, African slaves on the plantations of East Texas, Hispanics in the Lower Rio Grande Valley, German immigrants in the Hill Country, and subsistence farmers of Scots-Irish descent all had their own meat-cooking styles. The meats were equally varied, including beef, pork, mutton, goat, venison, squirrel, and any number of others. When the Texas cattle industry emerged after the war, beef became cheap and commonly available, and it was soon a central part of everybody's cooking. But beef is hardly the whole story.

Texans barbecue pork.

When visitors from the Carolinas and Tennessee come to Texas, they are generally astonished to find that we eat a lot of pork here as well as beef brisket. That's the problem with the beef generalization. Yes, we barbecue beef brisket, but we're also fond of other cuts. East Texas barbecue is a proud variant of the African-American Southern barbecue tradition, and although both consider pork their crowning glory, cooks in East Texas have their own way of doing things. Southern pork would never be served without barbecue sauce, but some East Texans like slow-smoked pork ribs with a little salt and pepper—and not a speck of sauce.

Texans barbecue sausage.

Now there's a Texas barbecue item you don't hear much about. The concept of barbecued sausage seems to have originated in the state's German belt in the 1800s. The smoked sausage produced by Czech and German meat markets in that area would have been virtually indistinguishable from the smoked sausage that butchers produced in central Europe.

Who decided it was barbecue? It was most likely one of those accidents that occur when cultures bump into one another. Itinerant farmworkers discovered the smoked meats in German butcher shops and, in the absence of any better explanation, they declared it to be barbecue. So it was.

And smoked sausage is still considered barbecue in every hamlet in the old German belt—from Smolik's in Cuero to City Market in Schulenburg to Dozier's Grocery in Fulshear. Little combination meat markets and barbecue joints crank out an endless variety of smoked sausages: links, rings, and uncut coils; garlic sausage; German sausage with mustard seeds; all-pork sausage; all-beef sausage; sage sausage; Czech sausage with coarse black pepper; wet sausage; beef and pork sausage; and, of course, the perennial favorite, Elgin hot guts.

Texans barbecue cows' heads.

This tradition traces its origins back to the Mexican *barbacoa* style, only it evolved into something completely different in Texas. Now, you might say that a cow's head cooked in an oven isn't really barbecue. But then you would have to define barbecue, which is always a tricky proposition.

Grilled shish kebab? Grilled salmon steaks? That's not barbecue in Texas—but smoked bologna is. It's served at the Railhead Smokehouse in Fort Worth. Steaks on the gas grill? No way! But what if you cook a double-cut sirloin over mesquite coals in an enclosed pit?

Sure! That's the way it's done at Cooper's in Llano—definitely a legitimate style of Texas barbecue.

Confused yet? Good, because that's just the tip of the iceberg. I think it's fair to say that Texas has more variations in its barbecue styles than any other state. And more disagreements about them.

Truth be told, Texans barbecue all kinds of things in lots of different ways.

This book wasn't written to claim some kind of barbecue supremacy for Texas. Tennessee, the Carolinas, and other states have fine barbecue, and most Texans enjoy it when they visit those places. The intention of this book is to offer a broader view of what barbecue really means across the Lone Star State. And to give a little recognition to the African-Texans, Mexican-Texans, German-Texans, and Anglo cowboys and farmers whose culinary traditions have melded to form the cultural icon that is modern Texas barbecue.

I hope these recipes and tips preserve a little Texas folklore and also serve as an invitation to join in and barbecue Texas-style in your own backyard. Please enjoy this book exactly the way it was written—in the shade of a tall tree with the smoker going.

Women outside Louie Mueller
Barbecue, Taylor, 1982.
Photo by Michael Murphy

Roasting meats on the barbecue (circa 1900).

LEGENDARY BARBECUE

The Evolution of the Pit

Forty-two cattle were barbecued for a "Get Together" to bring farmers and townspeople together, Victoria, 1921. (Note the axles used as crossbars.)

he pitmaster squints into the smoke as he opens the giant steel door. From your place in line, you watch him fork and flip the juicy, black beef clods and sizzling pork loins. Your heart beats faster as he reveals a dozen sausage rings hissing and spitting in the thick white cloud. Slowly, the sweet oak smoke makes its way to you, carrying with it the aroma of peppery beef, bacon-crisp pork, and juicy garlic sausage. Your mouth starts watering.

You swallow hard. Your stomach rears back and lets out a growl. You're in a frenzy by the time you get to the head of the line, where the hot meats are being sliced and weighed. You order twice as much as you can eat. You carry it away on a sheet of butcher paper, with an extra sheet tucked underneath for a plate.

Welcome to Texas barbecue. We love to eat it. We love to make it. And we love to argue about it. We have competing theories on the etymology and the definition of the word and on which characteristics make it uniquely Texan. We don't agree on the kind of wood, the need for sauce, the cut of meat, or which part of the state does it best. And we all have our favorite pitmasters. But we all agree that non-Texans don't understand it.

Pitmaster Roy Perez at the
old Kreuz Market.
Photo by Wyatt McSpadden

Men in suits waiting for barbecued mutton cooking on an open pit, 1921.

Traditional barbecue definitions don't make sense here. "Barbecue is always served with a distinctive sauce," say some. Not in Texas, where the sauce is on the side and many connoisseurs elect to eat their smoked meats with no sauce at all. "Barbecue means slow cooking over the low heat of a wood or charcoal fire," say others. Sorry. Some of the best smoked meat in the Lone Star State is cooked at 500°F.

So what is Texas barbecue exactly? If we can't quite agree on what it is, at least we can agree on where it came from. Looking at Texas barbecue history may be the easiest way to understand it.

If you include roasting meat on an open fire in your definition of barbecue, then the earliest Texans to barbecue were the Caddo Indians, who cooked venison and other game here thousands of years ago. They were followed by the Spanish shepherds, who spit-roasted kid goat and lamb *al pastor* (shepherd style) on the South Texas plains, starting in the 1600s. Mexican barbacoa, meat sealed in maguey leaves and buried in a *pozo* (pit) full of hot rocks, was common in South Texas before the earliest Anglo settlers began to arrive in the 1820s. In modified forms, it can still be found today at barbacoa eateries like Vera's Backyard Bar-B-Que in Brownsville.

The largest influx of Southerners was the group called the Old Three Hundred, 297 primarily wealthy plantation owners who, in 1824, populated Stephen F. Austin's colony, which he had acquired through a Mexican colonization grant. Attracted by the rich soil of the river bottom lands of the Brazos Valley, these cotton planters replicated the culture of the Old South in Texas, including Southern-style barbecue. They brought their slaves with them, and African-Americans became the earliest pitmasters in Texas, just as they had been in the rest of the South.

Pits were typically three feet deep, twenty-five feet long, and three feet across. Whole sheep, goats, pigs, and steers were slaughtered on the spot, cut into pieces, and cooked over oak or hickory coals while being continuously basted. The standard cooking time was twenty-four hours. Southern-style pit barbecue can still be seen today in the community barbecues held in Austin County, not far from the area where Austin's colony was once headquartered.

The earliest mention of Texas barbecue in print is from an 1832 handbill advertising a Shelby County revival meeting, where free barbecue

Civic Barbecues

Big public barbecues were held for all kinds of reasons in the early days of the Lone Star State. In fact, no civic celebration was complete without one.

In 1853, the town of Stafford gave away free barbecue to the public to celebrate becoming a stop on the Buffalo Bayou, Brazos and Colorado Railway.

In 1860, Sam Houston spoke at the Great American Barbecue, a political rally thrown by the American Party in Austin. All citizens of the state were invited to attend and eat for free.

In 1891, the citizens of Whitney, a town with a declining population, held a barbecue to promote the benefits of citizenship. They gave away thirty-five hundred pounds of barbecue.

In 1926, Edgar Byram Davis closed what was probably the biggest oil deal in the state up to that time. He got $12 million (half of it in cash) for his Luling oil holdings, and he held a free barbecue to celebrate. Attendance estimates run as high as thirty-five thousand.

In 1941, at his inauguration celebration, Governor W. Lee "Pappy" O'Daniel set up pits on the grounds of the capitol building in Austin and gave away barbecue to all comers.

In 1964, President Lyndon Johnson hosted the president-elect of Mexico at a state dinner at the LBJ Ranch in Johnson City. Catered by Walter Jetton, this dinner for two hundred fifty was reportedly America's first official barbecue state dinner.

In 1991, the pitmasters at XIT Rodeo and Reunion in Dalhart cooked eleven thousand pounds of beef in open pits dug with backhoes. The meat was served to twenty thousand guests. The XIT barbecue is still held every year.

Overview of the crowd at the barbecue on the state capitol grounds
celebrating Governor "Pappy"
O'Daniel's inauguration in 1941.
The large circles are cowboy hats,
the little white circles are plates.

Governor W. Lee "Pappy' O'Daniel poses with a mop while pretending to cook barbecue in an open pit on the capitol grounds during his inauguration celebration, 1941.

was handed out to all comers. Barbecue had become an integral part of the Protestant religious rallies that began in the late 1700s in Kentucky and spread religion across the frontier. The camp meetings were usually held from Thursdays through Sundays, with free barbecue all weekend.

Old-world meat smoking was brought to Central Texas by German and Czech butchers during an era of intense European migration that began in the 1830s and reached its height around 1890. The German meat markets sold fresh meats and smoked their leftovers in enclosed smokers, as they had done in the Old Country. They were probably astonished when migrant farmworkers began the tradition of eating that smoked meat on the spot. When food cooked in earthen pits was judged unsanitary by early health inspectors after the reforms of the Progressive Era in the early 1900s, the indoor German smokers became the model for barbecue restaurants. Which is why many people consider the old meat markets to be quintessential Texas barbecue joints, despite the fact that German smoked meats and sausages aren't really American barbecue.

Texas departed from the Southern "pork only" tradition, as well. After the Civil War, beef became the meat most characteristic of Texas barbecue. In the days before refrigeration, barbecuing beef meant getting enough people together to make killing a whole steer worthwhile. When that happened, it was quite a party. Although the ultimate in Southern barbecue was cooking a whole hog, cooking a whole steer was the ultimate in Texas barbecue.

Because you could feed so many people with a whole steer, Texas barbecues started out big—and then they got bigger. Texans being Texans, barbecues became competitions, and each barbecue became an effort to outdo all others. This tradition lives on in such events as the XIT Rodeo and Reunion in Dalhart, where tens of thousands of people gather each year to attend the "world's largest free barbecue."

The Barbecue Barons

Walter Jetton of Fort Worth was the single most influential figure in Texas barbecue history. For many years, Jetton held the record for barbecue catering, having fed twelve thousand people at one of his "chuck wagon dinners."

During Lyndon Johnson's presidency, Jetton became nationally famous for his barbecues at the LBJ ranch. In 1965, Pocket Books published *Walter Jetton's LBJ Barbecue Cook Book*. In the book he advised: "To barbecue, you need a pit . . . This doesn't have to be a hole in the ground, and it definitely shouldn't be one of those backyard creations with

Linguistic Lore
BQ

Over the years, some pretty fantastic etymologies for the word *barbecue* have been advanced. Two cookbooks I've seen recount the tale of a wealthy Texas rancher who fed all of his friends whole sheep, hogs, and cattle roasted over open pits. In one cookbook, the rancher's name is Bernard Quayle, and in the other, it is Barnaby Quinn, but both describe the branding iron of the ranch as having the initials B. Q. with a straight line underneath. Texas ranches are named for their brands, and a straight line is called a bar. Thus, the "bar B. Q." became synonymous with fine eating—or so the story goes.

The late Corpus Christi barbecue legend Joe Cotten used to tell journalists that the word *barbecue* came from the French phrase *barbe à queue*, meaning "from the beard to the tail." The phrase supposedly refers to the fact that the whole animal is roasted. The reporters passed along Joe's wisdom to many readers, and this explanation is still widely circulated. The *Oxford English Dictionary* calls this particular etymology "absurd conjecture."

Legendary Fort Worth barbecuer Walter Jetton.

a chimney." A fire built in a cinder block enclosure was perfect in his view.

But Jetton actually had two different barbecue styles—one for catering and another at his eponymous restaurant in Fort Worth. For chuck wagon events, Jetton cooked meat outdoors in cinder-block pits directly over the coals for eighteen to twenty-four hours. But that wouldn't work in a restaurant.

County health departments regulate barbecue pits in Texas food service establishments. The regulations, and how strictly they are enforced, have varied widely from county to county since the laws first hit the books during the sanitation crusades of the Progressive Era in the early 1900s.

The brick smokers of the old German-belt meat markets, some built more than a hundred years ago, offered a design that was adopted by other barbecue restaurants once the outdoor pits were outlawed. But the mystique of African-American barbecue pitmasters continued—some restaurants proudly advertised that they had black pitmasters manning the indoor barbecue pits.

In a 1956 story in the Saturday Evening Post titled "He's the Kingpin of the Barbecuemen," Jetton introduced the reporter to an African-American pitmaster named Ethan Boyer, "a dignified, sixty-year-old Negro" who supervised cooking in the brick pits at the restaurant. Jetton called Boyer, who had been with him for thirty years, his "barbecue expert."

Mechanization

In 1946, a machinist named Leonard McNeill won a tiny restaurant near Lenox Street in Houston in a game of craps. He renamed it the Lenox Bar-B-Q. By the 1960s, the restaurant was catering for thousands of guests at a time, and McNeill found himself competing head to head with the legendary Walter Jetton. In 1967, Ann Valentine, food editor of the *Houston Post*, wrote an article about the two mega-caterers titled "The Barbecue Barons."

McNeill prepared food at a restaurant, where he had to abide by the sanitary codes. But ordinary brick barbecue smokers couldn't accommodate jobs the size of those that the Lenox Bar-B-Q was being asked to do. So the machinist-turned–barbecue baron introduced barbecue to the age of mechanization.

McNeill bought an enormous bread-rising oven from the Rainbow Bread bakery. The oven had a rotating mechanism inside that moved the dough through a timed cycle. McNeill converted this machinery into a mechanized wood-smoke rotisserie that could cook three thousand pounds of meat at one time.

Today, what's left of McNeill's barbecue joint on Harrisburg Boulevard in Houston is run by Erik Mrok, whose father was a friend of McNeill's. Construction of Houston's light rail line forced Lenox Barbecue & Catering, as it is now known, to move out of its dining room, which was bulldozed. The restaurant kitchen still uses rotisserie ovens to produce barbecue for take-out and catering.

Linguistic Lore
BABRACOT

According to the *Oxford English Dictionary* entry, the English word *barbecue* derives from the Spanish word *barbacoa*, which is in turn a variation of *babracot*, a word that comes to us from the Taíno language, part of the Arawakan language family of the Caribbean. In Taíno, however, the term *babracot* was used for the framework of green sticks that formed the grill, rather than for the cooking itself.

The Caribbean style of slow smoking on a grate over coals was brought to the Carolinas by African slaves in the 1600s and became the basis for Southern-style barbecue. Advocates of open-pit barbecue once argued that this was the only true barbecue. But nowadays, German-style meat smoked in an enclosed pit, Mexican *cabrito al pastor* roasted by an open fire, and ribs grilled over direct heat all fall within somebody's definition of Texas barbecue.

All Texans agree, however, that hamburgers and hot dogs are not barbecue.

Mr. White. A roadside barbecue
stand operator in Palestine, 1981.
Photo by Scott Van Osdol

The barbecue rotisseries are of a type patented by Herbert Oyler in 1968. Oyler, who owned a barbecue restaurant in Mesquite, also started by tinkering with a barbecue rotisserie made from a bread-rising oven. Whether he was working independently, in competition, or in cooperation with McNeill is not known.

Oyler's invention is a steel barbecue pit with a rotisserie inside. It has an electric carousel, though no heating elements. It is fueled exclusively with wood burned in a remote firebox. The advantage of the rotisserie is that the meat gets basted with dripping fat, but it is cooked with wood smoke. Although it isn't exactly an old-fashioned barbecue pit, the results still depend on time, temperature, and the talent of the pitmaster. Oyler pits, made today by J&R Manufacturing, are used by well-known barbecue establishments throughout the state. Bewley pits, made by A. N. Bewley in Dallas, are similar in design.

The Portable Pit

The oil business, which took off in the 1950s, had a big impact on Texas barbecue. Oilmen were not only notoriously fond of smoked meat but also fascinated by barbecue technology.

The backyard charcoal grill of the 1960s was fine for grilling steaks, hamburgers, and hot dogs, but it wasn't suited to Texas barbecue. In the 1970s and 1980s, a larger, enclosed style of barbecue smoker began to proliferate.

It's not hard to figure out where these Texas-style portable pits came from. Some of them were just oil drums cut in half, with legs and handles welded on. Others were elaborate affairs with multiple smoke chambers, separate fireboxes, chimneys, flues, and grease drains. But all of them were made from oil-field parts.

"We made the chambers out of used oil pipe. You didn't want to know what used to be in your barbecue pit in those days," laughs Wayne Whitworth, founder of Houston's Pitt's & Spitt's, one of the most famous makers of barbecue equipment in Texas.

"We were metal fabricators; we did big oil-field contracts. We just built barbecue pits for fun," Whitworth says. There were a lot of barbecue enthusiasts working in the East Texas oil fields. And with all that welding equipment and those parts just lying around, temptation was hard to resist. "If you had all the money it has cost Brown & Root [an oil-field engineering firm] to build barbecue pits, you could feed the world," Whitworth chuckles.

Although making barbecue pits was once a hobby for the oilman, it became a successful new career. In the early 1980s, when the price of oil fell from thirty dollars a barrel to under ten dollars, the Texas economy went into a tailspin. "In 1983, when oil went to hell, I had my workers making barbecue pits just to keep them busy," Whitworth remembers.

"Nowadays, we can't keep up with the demand," Whitworth says. "We don't use old pipe anymore; we use new steel these days. And we can build them as big or as small as you want them." Pitt's & Spitt's is now run by Robert Smith and Ryan Zboril, and the company shows off its new designs at barbecue cook-offs all over the country.

Stainless Steel and Gas

The invention of the high-tech stainless-steel barbecue oven heated by gas or electricity made opening a barbecue joint easy. A few logs are added for smoke, and the cooking process is electronically controlled. The ovens are convenient, they require no expertise to operate, and they avoid problems with air-pollution regulations.

The easy-bake oven of the barbecue world turned barbecue into fast food and gave rise to chains, franchise operations, and a host of mediocre barbecue joints located in shopping centers, in strip malls, and at highway exits across Texas and the rest of the South.

In order to compete with other strip-mall restaurants, modern barbecue joints offered barbecue at any time of the day, which meant the cooked meats were held in steam tables or ovens for hours. When the meat ran out, refrigerated barbecue cooked the day before was reheated and sliced. The result was a general decline in the quality of Texas barbecue.

Back to the Basics

Recently, a back-to-the-roots movement in Texas barbecue has captured the attention of barbecue lovers across the country. A handful of young pitmasters is going back to the basics in hip, new barbecue joints in major cities across the state. They are the darlings of the national press, and the luscious new style of meats they're serving is reviving the reputation of Texas barbecue.

Austin's Aaron Franklin is the best-known of the bunch. In 2015, he became the first barbecue pitmaster to win a James Beard Award, an honor given to the nation's top chefs. Franklin Barbecue in Austin was named the best barbecue joint in the country by *Bon Appétit* in 2011.

A second-generation barbecue man (his parents once owned a barbecue joint in Bryan), Franklin pioneered the trend of buying premium meat, charging higher prices, and serving a new style of barbecue. This brisket is fattier, has a crispy bark, is cooked to over 200°F, and is sliced as it's served. Franklin is also expanding the genre. He not only serves a Southern-style pulled pork sandwich but also tops his pork and chopped brisket sandwiches with Carolina-style coleslaw.

Justin Fourton at Pecan Lodge in the Deep Ellum area of Dallas is famous for his Fred Flintstone–size beef ribs: a single rib weighs 1½ pounds or more and sells for as much as thirty dollars (see page 245). His wife, Diane, makes Southern sides like collard greens and a banana pudding inspired by her aunt's recipes.

Ronnie Killen at Killen's Barbecue in Pearland, a southern suburb of Houston, is also known for USDA Prime brisket, giant beef ribs, pulled pork, pork belly, and home-style side dishes like creamed corn made from fresh corn off the cob.

The CorkScrew BBQ trailer in north Houston is run by the husband-and-wife team of Will and Nichole Buckman, who, not too long after opening, found themselves installing a new J&R Oyler smoker with an eighteen-hundred-pound capacity to keep up with the demand.

What all of these places have in common are expensive grades of meat, wood-burning pits, fattier brisket with crunchy bark—and long lines of 'cue hounds waiting for the kitchen to open. The line isn't just a sign of popularity, however. Aaron Franklin suggests that having people waiting in line is critical to the quality of the barbecue.

When every bit of meat is carved as it is ordered, fresh off the smoker, every customer gets a juicy slice. That's the way it was done years ago, before high-tech barbecue existed. Just ask Vencil Mares at Taylor Cafe. The dean of Texas pitmasters slices his brisket just like he did when the place first opened in 1948—with a layer of fat on top. "You cut that fat off and you're cutting all the seasonings off," he told barbecue writer Daniel Vaughn.

The move away from fatty barbecue was part of the same national trend that replaced butter with margarine in the middle of the last century. In 1952, in Fort Worth's *Star-Telegram*, Texas writer J. Frank Dobie observed that "the barbecuers of restaurants . . . all agree that in recent years demand for lean meat

is making men and women alike into Jack Sprats. Fat meat is much more easily barbecued than lean meat, and the old-timers all wanted fat meat. Young people nowadays don't want fat, and lots not young don't either."

While the new breed of pitmasters is getting a lot of press, they prepare only a tiny percentage of the barbecue consumed in Texas. But lots of traditional barbecue joints have taken notice, so that more and more pitmasters are offering a choice of lean meat or brisket with the fat attached. And you don't even have to queue up to get it.

Who is willing to wait in line for a plate of fatty barbecue? You probably won't be surprised to hear that it's the same gang of hipster food lovers who made *chashu* ramen, Wagyu hamburgers, and all kinds of pork belly dishes popular.

According to the new "fat means flavor" thinking, fatty barbecue tastes better, too. Fatty end brisket, incredibly marbled beef ribs, and the new Southern-style pulled pork are what hip young barbecue customers are after. We have come full circle. In the 1950s, it was the young customers who demanded leaner barbecue; in the early twenty-first century, it is the young customers who think "fat is where it's at."

Austin pitmaster Aaron Franklin.

WHAT I LEARNED AT BARBECUE SUMMER CAMP

Hands-on meat-cutting demonstration at Barbecue Summer Camp.

arbecue Summer Camp and its winter counterpart, Camp Brisket, are annual weekend-long barbecue seminars. Created by Foodways Texas, a nonprofit headquartered at the University of Texas at Austin, in cooperation with the Texas A&M Meat Science Center, a part of the Texas A&M University Department of Animal Science, the seminars touch on barbecue culture and history before delving deep into butchering and barbecue cookery.

There are hands-on classes in equipment, fuels, seasonings, cooking techniques, food safety, and elementary cattle and hog anatomy. Classes are taught by professors of the meat science center, top Texas pitmasters, and experts from Foodways Texas. At lunchtime, attendees eat what they cook—and some of the dinners are catered by the best barbecue joints in the state.

Barbecue Summer Camp and Camp Brisket both feature an early-morning demonstration of barbecue rigs and the latest in hardware. Everything from simple Webers and barrel smokers to the most elaborate cook-off competition trailers are there to play with.

HOME BARBECUE RIGS

You don't have to spend a lot of money on equipment to make great-tasting barbecue. If, however, you *are* in the mood to spend a lot of money, there's a really cool barbecue rig out there with your name on it. Here are some ideas as to what's available.

WEBER

While there are several bullet-shaped water smokers on the market, the Weber Smokey Mountain Cooker is the only one that comes highly recommended. It's a water smoker with a large water pan and a steel door on the side to allow refueling. The 18½-inch size is just big enough to handle a brisket; the 22½-inch size can accommodate even more meat.

Cook-off competitors have won contests with Weber Smokey Mountain water smokers, but only after making a few adjustments. After-market suppliers sell replacement grill thermometers (see Thermometers, page 58), gaskets to improve the seal on the fuel door, a hinge to hold the lid up, and extensions to raise the height of the cooker, along with lots of other intriguing gizmos. Weber products are widely available.
CONTACT: weber.com 800-446-1071.

BARRELS (TEXAS HIBACHIS OR BIG UGLY BARRELS)

From the first time I went to Kreuz Market and saw those big oak logs blazing, I dreamed of the day when I could start burning hardwood myself. Wood chips are fine, but I wanted a real barbecue unit—something I could throw logs into—so I bought my first barrel smoker. Also known as a Texas hibachi, a barrel smoker is a 55-gallon metal drum turned on its side and sawed in half. Legs and handles are welded onto it to make it easy to use. A barrel smoker gives you enough room to burn hardwood, or at least to throw a few logs onto a charcoal fire. If you get two or three years out of a barrel smoker, you're doing fine. The tops never close evenly, the grills burn through, and sooner or later the barrel rusts out or the welds break, which is probably why barrel smokers are not shipped to other parts of the country.

Because the fuel sits directly on the floor of the barrel, the fire can be hard to start and quick to go out. That's why I added a smaller rectangular grate on the bottom of the barrel. It's a 12-by-18-inch length of extended metal and it sits about 3 inches off the bottom, improving the airflow significantly.

Some of the top cook-off competitors in the state swear that the Texas hibachi is the perfect barbecue unit. Many similar barbecue rigs are available, often made out of sheet metal but designed on the same premise: the fire is on one end and the meat is on the other. With a few adjustments (like adding a fuel grate), these smokers work great.

CONTACT: Found outside of grocery stores, hardware stores, and feed stores; also available as a do-it-yourself kit for home welders.

OFFSET BARBECUE PITS

For my fortieth birthday, my former wife bought me a big, black, heavy-gauge-steel barbecue pit made by Smoke-master. The firebox and grill are on one side, and a separate smoke chamber big enough to hold a brisket, five pounds of sausage, and a couple of chickens is on the other side. The smoke chamber has a built-in thermometer on top, and there is a drain plug for cleaning on the bottom. Underneath the grill is a drawer to remove the ashes, and the chimney has a damper to control the smoke flow. You can grill in it, you can smoke in it, you can burn all the logs you want. It cost $650 back then; similar units now sell for around $1,500. My pit is more than twenty years old and in use constantly, so you have to figure that a pit like this is an excellent investment. Smokemaster went out of business, but there are other makers out there. Offset pits made of thin sheet metal are quite a bit cheaper, but they don't last very long.

CONTACT: Pitt's & Spitt's at 800-521-2947 or www.pittsandspitts.com for a catalog; or BBQ pits by KLOSE at 800-487-7487.

BARBECUE TRAILERS

A barbecue trailer is a giant smoker on wheels, complete with a trailer hitch, brake lights, and Texas license plates. My daughters, Katie and Julia, have birthdays a few days apart in early April. When Katie turned four and Julia turned two, we had a huge birthday party to which we invited over a hundred people. Of course, the two toddlers couldn't have cared less about the whole affair, except for the piñata. It was really just a good excuse to rent a barbecue trailer. For the two days that the trailer was parked in the driveway, with its giant counterweighted steel doors and a quarter cord of aged oak stacked neatly along its edge, I was in barbecue heaven. I cooked a whole *cabrito* (baby goat), four briskets, ten pounds of venison sausage I had stuffed myself, and a couple of pork butts. Then I smoked a big ham to have the next weekend for Easter.

You can get a barbecue trailer at many rental centers in Texas, provided your pickup has a trailer hitch. You see barbecue trailers at shade-tree barbecue stands by the side of the road, at catered events, and at barbecue cook-offs.

Barbecue cook-off teams build their own custom trailers and take them on the road for the summer cook-off circuit. Some of them are pretty impressive. Pitts & Spitts demonstrates a trailer with built-in fans wired to an electronic thermostat, so that when the heat gets too low, the fans kick in. Now that's a great combination of high and low tech.

CONTACT: Pitt's and Spitt's at 800-521-2947 or www.pittsandspitts.com for a catalog.

BRICK AND MASONRY PITS

The Saturday night meal at Barbecue Summer Camp is a whole-hog roast held in Dr. Jeff Savell's backyard. Sausage and sides are usually provided by a famous barbecue joint, and Shiner donates the beer.

Dr. Savell has constructed a cinder-block pit large enough to hold a whole hog. It measures 2½ blocks (40 inches) wide and 6½ blocks (104 inches) long. The cinder blocks are stacked but not mortared together, so the pit can be disassembled and relocated. A few of the blocks on the bottom are turned sideways to create a controllable draft. The pit has a stainless-steel lid and a steel rack with handles that sits inside, both supplied by a friendly metal fabricator.

An outdoor smoker made of brick or cinder block is the ultimate in barbecue pits, provided that it is properly designed. If you are going to build one, make sure you start with plans that will allow you to control the heat and smoke.

Houston home barbecuer Ricky Adams samples some meat from a barrel smoker in his front yard.

There are several modern pieces of equipment that we don't cover at Barbecue Summer Camp. Here's a quick run-down.

COLD SMOKERS Once upon a time, when iceboxes had enamel interiors, discarded refrigerators were used as cold smokers. You inserted one of those electric charcoal lighters through a hole drilled in the bottom on one side and stacked some hardwood chips on it. Then you put some meat on the shelves, plugged in the charcoal starter, and shut the door. The door sealed the smoke inside, and your food got a smoky flavor fast. To finish, you cooked the meat in the oven or on a grill.

You can do something similar with a stove-top smoker, a sealed stainless-steel container that works on a home cooktop. You sprinkle hardwood sawdust in the bottom, place the food on a rack, seal the container, put it on a burner, and turn on the heat. The sawdust smolders in the tightly sealed container without stinking up the house, and your food is smoked in minutes.

The Camerons stove-top smoker, which is made by a company in Colorado, comes outfitted with apple, alder, cherry, hickory, maple, mesquite, oak, and pecan "smoke dust." It works great on half a chicken, a couple of sausage links, or a piece of fish. But you can't cook a brisket or a rack of ribs on it.

CONTACT: Camerons Professional Cookware at 888-563-0227 or www.cameronssmoker.com.

GAS GRILLS Forget it. You can't smoke meat on a gas grill. I've tried those little metal boxes that are supposed to hold smoldering wood chips. I've even tried putting the chips on aluminum foil. It just doesn't work.

PELLET SMOKERS These automated barbecue units, which burn sawdust pellets, employ a thermostat and mechanized auger feeder that delivers the pellets into an electric heating element to maintain a preset heat level. At low temperatures, the pellets create a good bit of smoke. There is no grill surface and no way to sear or grill anything. Pellet smokers work reasonably well and appeal to folks who don't want to get involved with live-fire cooking.

Breaking It In

A brand new smoker straight from the manufacturer is going to burn too hot and emit unpleasant odors from the grease, metal shavings, and other residue left inside. To burn in your smoker, light a hot fire without any food inside and keep it burning for a couple of hours. After the smoker has cooled, wipe out any ash, rub the grate with vegetable oil, and you should be ready to cook. Consider buying a waterproof cover for your barbecue smoker to keep it from rusting. Lubricate the hinges frequently.

Grady Spears and his refrigerator smoker, Alpine, 1997.

Tools You'll Need

A stick to poke the coals and a fork to flip the meat were about all that was required to cook barbecue in the good old days. Today, we have come to rely on various modern conveniences; some have come to be considered absolute necessities while others are just handy gadgets— you'll have to decide for yourself which is which.

ALUMINUM FOIL
Lots of the recipes in this book call for you to wrap the meat in foil. You'll need the heavy-gauge, extra-wide variety.

ALUMINUM FOIL PANS
You may have used one of these large disposable pans to cook a turkey for Thanksgiving. They are most commonly available in rectangular shapes, including half sheet and full sheet. There is also a large oval pan, which is handy for whole cows' heads, if you're cooking barbacoa. Barbecue cook-off competitors use the pans to smoke chicken and other cuts to prevent the meats from burning and for smoke-braised recipes.

BUTCHER PAPER
Old-time Texas butchers use "peach paper" to wrap their meats. This uncoated food-grade paper is light pink in color, hence the name. Wrapping barbecue meats in butcher paper is a good alternative to wrapping them in aluminum foil. While foil-wrapped meat will continue to cook with lots of steam, paper-wrapped meat can still vent some moisture. You can use white, brown or peach-colored butcher paper (not kraft paper), but make sure to get untreated butcher paper that is approved for food service use. Some Texas barbecue joints use the greasy discarded paper from the previous day to start their fires the next morning.

CHARCOAL STARTER CHIMNEY
A charcoal starter chimney is a cylindrical container with a grate in the middle and a fireproof handle on the outside. You fill the top of the container with charcoal, stuff some newspaper in the bottom, and light the paper. Within ten minutes or so, you have hot coals without using any starter fluid. Some people use paraffin along with the newspaper, but it isn't necessary. Weber makes an extra-large chimney that suits me perfectly.

These chimneys became popular in California after the city of Los Angeles banned the use of charcoal starter fluid because it is an environmental menace. It's a culinary menace, too. If you're not careful, you end up with barbecue that smells like an oil refinery.

Note: Never put a lit chimney on a picnic table, deck, or other flammable surface.

CONTACT: Chimney starters are available anywhere barbecue equipment is sold.

DRIP PANS AND WATER PANS
A drip pan is a container placed under the meat to keep the fat from falling into the fire and flaring up. It is usually

filled with water or some other liquid (such as Lone Star beer). A water pan is a pan placed in the smoke chamber between the food and the fire. Its purpose is to keep a high level of moisture in the smoke chamber so the meat stays moist. In a water smoker like the Weber Smokey Mountain Cooker, a pan filled with water placed between the meat and the fire serves both purposes at once.

A water pan adds moisture to the cooking chamber; it's always a good idea if you have room for it. If your smoking chamber is so full of meat that a water pan won't fit, don't worry—the meat itself will emit moisture as it cooks. That's why it's a better idea to barbecue a lot of meat rather than a single cut. If you are cooking meat that is fatty, you may need to position a drip pan under the meat to keep the fire from flaring up. You will need to replenish the liquid in a water pan or drip pan as needed while you cook.

I use a metal baking pan for a water pan or drip pan, but I have accepted the fact that it will never be clean enough to bake a cake in again. Pyrex is a washable alternative, but disposable aluminum pans are perfect for this.

FLAVOR INJECTOR

It looks like a giant syringe, and that's actually what it is. You fill the chamber with a liquid marinade and inject it into the meat. Injecting is much more efficient than marinating or brining. There are many models available, starting at around $5 for a little plastic syringe. For $50, you can get a professional meat injector that looks like a paint gun—that's what we use to inject several gallons of brine into a whole hog at Barbecue Summer Camp.

GLOVES

Handling barbecue with fireproof or heat-resistant gloves not only prevents you from damaging the meat with utensils but is also generally easier and cuts down on burns. You can find them at some barbecue specialty shops. Fabric gloves get dirty fast. Barbecue competitors favor Neox gloves, which have a heat-resistant neoprene coating and a cotton lining and are washable.

KNIVES

Boning Knives: A 6-inch boning knife is the ideal tool to trim a brisket or a rack of ribs. You can find inexpensive models with plastic handles starting at around $25—and deluxe models for much more. Some pitmasters prefer the ones with curved tips for trimming briskets.

Carving Knives: Many cook-off competitors like electric knives, especially for meats that tear easily under the pressure of a regular slicing knife (like falling-apart-tender pork ribs). The meat science professors at Texas A&M recommend oversize slicing knives that are long enough to span a brisket—12 to 14 inches.

If you are looking for something traditional, go for the old-fashioned scimitar shape (tip curved upward), often seen in vintage barbecue joints. The modern

Roy Perez at the chopping block with his favorite knives.

favorite slicing knife for brisket is straight as a yardstick, with a rounded blunt tip and a Granton-style blade.

Granton is the name of the cutlery company, based in the United Kingdom, that patented the blade in 1928. Nowadays Granton, or the term *duo-edge,* has come to describe any knife with a straight blade and two identical rows of indentations on either side of the cutting edge. The dimples improve the performance of the knife by cutting down on surface contact, thus reducing the drag and "stickiness" of the blade. The long, dimpled blade is a favorite in delis, where it is used to slice smoked salmon paper-thin, but the long knife also produces clean, uniform slices of brisket without tearing even the tenderest meat.

Lots of companies sell similar knives, but a 12- to 14-inch slicer from the original Granton knife company is a bargain: it costs under $40 online, and for a few bucks more, you can get one with a rosewood handle.

Knife Sharpening Tools: While you are shopping for knives, don't forget about knife sharpening tools—they are available wherever knives are sold. You should be putting an edge on your knives every time you use them and getting them sharpened every few months or so, depending on how much wear they get. I prefer a ceramic "honing rod" to the old-fashioned steel for regular use. For the long-term maintenance, you will also have to decide whether to have your knives professionally sharpened, or do it yourself with one of the many available kits (www.knifemerchant.com).

MOP
The old-timers still prefer a little cotton mop for basting—the kind used for washing dishes—but oversize silicone basting brushes are fast replacing all other contenders.

POKER
You need something to move hot coals around. A stout stick from the yard will do.

SCRUB BRUSH
No, the black gunk stuck to the grill doesn't add flavor—not the good kind, anyway. Fire up your grill and clean the cooking surface with a heatproof scrubber every time you barbecue. Get rid of your wire brushes—these are a safety hazard—when the steel bristles fall out, as they can accidently become lodged in the meat and be ingested.

SPATULA
Look for a large, heavy-duty metal barbecue spatula anywhere that sells barbecue gear.

TONGS
Many cook-off competitors insist that continued forking causes meats to lose too much juice. The long barbecue tongs don't handle heavy things very well. I like the short, spring-loaded kind you can get at restaurant supply houses.

THERMOMETERS

Grill Thermometers: Like an oven thermometer for your barbecue smoker, these instruments tell you the cooking temperature at the grill surface. Most barbecue smokers come with a thermometer installed, but they tend to break—and some aren't very reliable to begin with. Fervent barbecue enthusiasts drill several holes in the doors of their smoker and add extra thermometers to give them a better idea of the entire range of temperatures inside the smoker.

If you want to add grill thermometers to your smoker, or replace one that's shot, consider getting some high-quality hardware. The Tel-Tru BQ300 Barbecue Thermometer is an excellent grill thermometer that's available online for $50 to $60. Don't forget to buy the $7 installation kit—it has the hardware you need to screw the gauge in place.

Of course, you can also gauge the grill surface temperature with an electronic sensor on a dual-purpose electronic thermometer.

Meat Thermometers: Old-school pitmasters judged the level of doneness by inserting a fork into the meat and testing how easily it came out. If it came out effortlessly, the meat was done. If the fork dragged or caught, the meat needed more time. I think it's fair to say that every pitmaster in Texas uses a thermometer these days (with the possible exception of ninety-something-year-old Vencil Mares at Taylor Cafe; see page 182).

Throw away your old-fashioned meat thermometer with the little round analog gauge on the top and get yourself an instant-read digital meat thermometer. You'll find lots of inexpensive models—starting at around $15—on the market. The Thermapen by ThermoWorks is the state of the art in instant-read digital barbecue thermometers. You don't have to stand there burning the hair off your arm to get a reading, as the temperature is displayed the second the tip is inserted into the meat. The meat science professors at Texas A&M carry these in quick-draw leather holsters attached to their belts. The Thermapen costs around $90. You can spend as much as you want on a holster.

Electronic Thermometers: There are lots of digital thermometers with probes on fireproof lead wires that allow you to monitor the heat level of your meat continuously. Maverick Industries was one of the first on the market with such thermometers and the company still makes several models. ThermoWorks, the makers of the Thermapen, sells the ThermaQ (model # 231-050), a continuous-read electronic thermometer with type K thermocouple fittings that can handle high heat levels. You can choose from a variety of probes, including a Thermapen probe and a grill surface sensor. A kit with two probes costs around $130. A Bluetooth version is said to be in the works.

The iGrill from Apple combines a two-probe electronic thermometer that attaches to your barbecue unit with a free smartphone app that picks up the thermometer signal on Bluetooth and displays the temperatures on your iPhone or iPad.

You can use the probes to show the internal temperatures of two different cuts of meat, or use one for the meat and one for the temperature inside the smoker. (The probe designed to read the temperature of the grill surface must be purchased separately.)

At Barbecue Summer Camp, we also use the iGrill feature that records a graph of the time and temperature during the entire cooking process. This is an excellent tool for understanding how to cook a brisket. For example, the graph illustrates "the stall," the temperature plateau that the brisket hits at around 160°F.

If your barbecue smoker is close enough to your bedroom, the iGrill allows you to monitor your overnight cook from the comfort of your bed. But many have complained that the range of the iGrill Bluetooth connection is too limited.

Fuels

Wood is the preferred fuel in Texas barbecue, but it's not always an easy matter to cook with it. On a big barbecue smoker with plenty of distance between the heat source and the meat, you can burn a clean wood fire and keep the cooking chamber at a low temperature. But you can't very well throw a log into your Weber Smokey Mountain. With smaller equipment, you have to learn to improvise with a combination of

charcoal, wood chunks, and wood chips. Here are a few suggestions.

CHARCOAL

Some barbecuers cook with charcoal, and some cook with wood, but most use a combination of the two. Cook-off veteran Harley Goerlitz recommends starting with charcoal and adding wood a little at a time.

Kingsford, or any other standard brand of pure charcoal briquette, will work fine. Avoid the cheap composite briquettes, which contain paraffin or petroleum by-products. Lump hardwood charcoal is the irregular kind that's not made into briquettes. Texas charcoal makers like B&B Charcoal, located in Weimar, market oak lump and other hardwood lump charcoals that provide some smoky flavor. They are popular for Southern-style whole-hog and open-pit cooking. Don't bother with the mesquite-flavored charcoal or other "flavored" briquettes. You want to use chips, chunks, or logs for smoke flavor.

WOOD

In Texas, the most popular barbecue woods are oak, pecan, hickory, and mesquite. Pitmasters tend to use the wood that is close at hand. That means post oak and pecan in Central Texas; pecan, red oak, and hickory in East Texas; and mesquite in South and West Texas.

In blind taste tests at Barbecue Summer Camp and Camp Brisket, attendees compare identical cuts of meat cooked over oak, mesquite, pecan, and hickory. The favorite for flavor in these experiments has alternated between hickory and oak, with pecan and mesquite consistently finishing third and fourth.

Pecan is a cousin of hickory. In fact, its original botanical name was *Hicoria pecan* (today, it is known as *Carya illinoinensis*). I have pecan trees in my yard, and I have some cut-up pecan on a wood pile next to the fence. When I want barbecue wood, I take a piece of wood from the pile and chop it into chunks that will fit into my firebox. If you have hickory, maple, alder, cherry, apple, oak, pecan, walnut, or some other hardwood tree in your neighborhood, you can do the same thing, but you have to season the wood first.

"Pecan tastes really sweet, but it's sooty—it makes the meat black," cook-off competitor Tommy Wimberly told me, "especially if it's a little green."

If you acquire freshly cut logs, it is a good idea to let them age for a year or two before using them. Kreuz Market in Lockhart keeps three woodpiles going. One pile is new post oak logs, another is year-old post oak logs, and the third is two-year-old post oak, which is mainly what they use for smoking.

Edgar Black Jr., down the street at Black's, mixes his woods. "We use the dry post oak for heat and some green post oak for smoke," he says. "If your meat is coming out too black, your wood is too green." Aaron Franklin of Franklin Barbecue in Austin recommends a "clean fire" of post oak that's burning, not smoldering.

At Snow's in Lexington, oak logs are burned down; the coals are shoveled into smokers; and pork, chicken, and ribs are placed on a grill about 26 inches above the coals—Snow's famous briskets are cooked with indirect heat in offset smokers burning post oak logs.

Mesquite is a completely different fuel. It is very resinous and burns hot. Grilling over mesquite is a great idea, but smoking with mesquite requires some adjustments. At Cooper's in Llano, the mesquite is burned down in a fireplace and then the glowing coals are shoveled into the smokers. This cuts down on the tar quite a bit. Cooper's also wraps its brisket in foil after several hours and continues cooking it on the coals.

Orange wood and peach wood are among the newest Texas barbecue fuels. They were recently introduced by WESTERN Premium BBQ Products in Pleasanton and are particularly well suited to chicken, turkey, and other mild-flavored meats.

Pitmaster Tootsie Tomanetz
at Snow's BBQ in Lexington.

Starting a Fire

A STARTER CHIMNEY HOLDS ABOUT TWENTY-FIVE BRIQUETTES, and that's how much I usually start with. As soon as you see flames coming out of the top of the chimney, dump the charcoal into the firebox or grate of your smoker. (If you forget to dump the charcoal, the chimney will quickly burn up all your fuel, and you'll have to start over.) You can start adding wood as soon as you dump the coals. If you are using lighter fluid, be sure to wait until the coals are white before you start cooking, so you don't get any lighter-fluid taste.

For a hot smoker, add another twenty-five briquettes once you get the first batch lit. This will bring you up to about 350°F very quickly. The bigger the pile of charcoal, the hotter the fire will burn.

To control the heat level, close down the dampers to lower the heat and stabilize the temperature. Then open the dampers a little at a time to increase the ventilation rate and raise the temperature. If your barbecue isn't drawing very well, consider making the chimney taller with rolled sheet metal or tin cans.

When you add wood chunks or logs to a charcoal fire, add them to the side rather than on top of the charcoal, so that they burn slowly at an even heat.

Direct and Indirect Heat Setups

COOKING OVER DIRECT HEAT Like open-pit cooking, cowboy-style barbecue calls for a good distance above the coals, to decrease the danger of burning. It's an easy way to cook a lot of meat at one time, and it doesn't take up much space. The biggest problem with cooking over direct heat is that you need a second fire so you'll have hot coals when you need to add them. (You can also use a starter chimney for this.)

To set up a grill for direct-heat cooking, spread hot coals evenly across the firebox and put the meat on the grill 18 inches or more above the coals.

COOKING OVER INDIRECT HEAT
Indirect heat has become the most common style of barbecue cooking. You can set up almost any barbecue cooker for indirect cooking by putting the fire on one side of the unit and the meat on the other. A drip pan is often positioned under the meat to prevent flare-ups.

SOME GENERAL TIPS
Keep your fuel dry and never soak the wood, as many sources suggest. Wet wood will just put the fire out. Always clean out all the old ashes before you start cooking and always clean the grill.

WEBER SMOKEY MOUNTAIN COOKER If you dump a lot of hot coals from a chimney into a Weber or smaller smoker, the fire tends to burn hot and then go out. That's fine for grilling, but not for barbecuing. For that reason, many barbecuers try to create fires that burn more slowly and evenly. The "Minion Method," named after a barbecuer named Jim Minion, starts with a small fire and adds coals around it. The "fuse method" calls for laying charcoal in the fire pan in a half circle and then putting lit coals onto one end so the coals light slowly and burn a little at a time, like a slow-burning fuse.

To start cooking, open the top vent all the way and open the bottom vents halfway. Lay out the charcoal in the bottom pan. Light ten briquettes of charcoal in a starter chimney and put the coals in the fuel pan. Fill the water pan with liquid. Put the meat over the water pan. (There is room for a second rack of meat in a 22½-inch model). Put wood chips on top of the charcoal as you cook to add smoke flavor. Control the temperature with the bottom air vents around the sides. Refuel as necessary.

BARREL SMOKERS (TEXAS HIBACHIS) Light a fire in one end of the barrel only. You can move the meat around to maintain a good cooking temperature. (You can also use a barrel for cowboy-style barbecue by putting the meat directly over the fire for all or part of the cooking time.) When using indirect heat, the part of the meat facing the fire will be the hottest, so rotate the meat regularly to keep it cooking evenly.

Small logs and charcoal are the safest fuels in a barrel. Flare-ups are a real problem. The fire can easily spread to the cooking meat and set your whole dinner ablaze, so be careful about how close you set the meat to the fire. Also, don't overload the grill with meat. Control the fire by opening and closing the chimney damper and fuel door to raise and lower the ventilation rate. Stick an oven thermometer inside for accuracy.

OFFSET BARBECUE PITS Before you begin, open the drain plug, drain out any old grease, and then rinse the smoke chamber with a hose. Be sure that ashes aren't preventing the ash drawer from closing completely and that the firebox lid and door close tightly. You need the air seal on your firebox to be as tight as possible. Excess ventilation will result in a fast-burning wood fire that will consume your fuel quickly and cook too hot.

Start a charcoal fire in a starter chimney, and pour the hot coals into the firebox. Add wood chunks or logs when you're ready to cook. Bring the fire up above the cooking temperature you need, and then close the dampers to reduce the heat. Try to maintain a steady heat. Continue opening and closing the firebox door and the chimney damper to raise and lower the ventilation rate and the temperature as needed.

Refuel as necessary, a minimum of at least once every hour and a half.

Cooking Temperatures

That Old Dogma Don't Hunt

In the days of the open pit, you had to cook low and slow or your meat would catch fire, so low and slow cooking (between 200° and 250°F) became part of barbecue dogma.

The most famous smoker in Texas has got to be the huge double-fireplace, high-chimney pit at the old Kreuz Market location in Lockhart (now Smitty's Market). Beef shoulder clods are cooked in this smoker for around four hours at temperatures as high as 500°F. The prime rib is barbecued in even less time. The design of smokers like this was the basis for the indirect method of cooking used in a Texas backyard barbecue rig, in which the firebox is separated from the smoke

chamber. Most of the recipes in this book call for temperatures between 225° and 300°F, but some go as high as 350°F. Most backyard smokers can handle this temperature without any problem.

"You want to cook your better cuts of beef faster and at higher temperatures," says John Fullilove, one-time pitmaster at Smitty's and at Schmidt Family Barbecue in Bee Cave. "Tough cuts like brisket have to cook slowly."

A barbecue pit is much like an oven. It can be set to many different temperatures. A brisket needs to simmer slowly in its own juices to get tender. In contrast, there's no reason to simmer a standing rib roast. It's easier to burn things at higher temperatures, so you have to be careful. Fullilove suggests that you pick the heat level that's right for the cut of meat you're cooking—and not worry about the dogma.

HOW TO TELL WHEN IT'S DONE

Veteran pitmasters can tell when the meat is done by poking it with a fork, and I once used this time-honored method myself. But now that I own a Thermapen instant-read digital thermometer, I use it every chance I get.

Several changes in the target temperature for barbecue have taken place recently. Disgruntled cooks who were tired of serving burnt meat were delighted when the United States Department of Agriculture (USDA) revised its standards. The recommended internal temperature for poultry was changed from 185°F to a more reasonable 165°F.

In fact, most cook-off competitors in the chicken category aim for 165°F at the breast and 175°F in the thickest part of the thigh.

The recommended internal temperature for pork went from 170°F to 145°F, the same temperature suggested for beef and lamb. This is an excellent target temperature for tender cuts like pork tenderloin and pork loin roast, especially if you like your pork a little pink.

Some changes have also been made on the other end of the spectrum, though not because the USDA changed its standards but rather because pitmasters began experimenting with new cooking techniques. Pulled pork is now considered done at 200°F, instead of the previous 190°F. And Texas pitmasters like Aaron Franklin are cooking their briskets to the once unheard-of temperature of 203°F.

Oversmoking

When you first get started with real-wood barbecuing, there is a tendency to oversmoke foods. It's not hard to tell when meat has been oversmoked, because it tastes like tar.

Resinous wood like mesquite; green, unseasoned woods; and wood that has been soaked in water can sometimes generate too much tarry smoke. If you cook with a blend of charcoal and wood or with dry seasoned wood, you shouldn't have this problem. But be aware that there is such a thing as too much smoke.

When to Use the Oven

Cook-off competitors are required to cook everything on the pit—and that's where the home cook has an advantage. When it starts raining, it gets dark, or you run out of firewood, there is no disgrace in finishing your barbecue in the oven. Once you've gotten a nice smoky flavor and a good grill char on your meat, it will taste just as good (or sometimes better) if you finish cooking it inside. Plus, finishing your barbecue in the oven is often a good way to avoid oversmoking it.

Just set your oven to the temperature specified in the recipe, transfer your meat, and follow the usual instructions. To hold meat that has already been cooked, wrap it in untreated butcher paper or aluminum foil and put it in a roasting pan in the oven at its lowest setting.

THE SPORT OF BARBECUE

Tips from the Trophy Winners

A competitor at the Houston Livestock Show and Rodeo Barbecue Cook-Off checks his brisket about an hour before the judging begins.

or the smoke-seasoned competitors who tow their barbecue trailers across Texas each summer, barbecue is more than a cooking style; it's a way of life. In Texas alone, more than one hundred barbecue cook-offs are held each year. Winners of regional cook-offs are invited to compete in national championships, such as the Kansas City Barbeque Society's American Royal Invitational in Kansas City, Missouri, and the Jack Daniel's Invitational in Lynchburg, Tennessee.

Drinking beer and watching meat smoke may seem like an odd competitive sport. Of course, it is a blind tasting of the smoked meat that determines the winner. At a regional cook-off, the judges sit together at picnic tables, and each one gets a ballot sheet. Twelve to fourteen numbered Styrofoam dishes full of meat are then passed around the table and scored. The judges are not allowed to express any opinions or to discuss the entries until the judging is complete.

Each contest has slightly different rules. At the Taylor International Barbecue Cook-Off, the samples get a simple 1 to 10 score. At another cook-off that I used to judge, the ballot is weighted, with appearance

Texas Pride at the Taylor International Barbecue Cook-Off.

and aroma each accounting for 5 points maximum, and taste and tenderness accounting for up to 20 points.

There's a lot to learn from the pitmasters at famous old Texas barbecue joints. Their opinions and unique regional styles are explored in the chapters that follow. But for the amateur point of view, it's hard to beat a barbecue cook-off. The pitmasters of the barbecue teams that consistently win the big contests may be the best teachers when it comes to backyard barbecue basics, if you can get them to talk to you. And that's generally a pretty big *if.*

Much has changed since my first gig as a judge at the 1996 Taylor International Barbecue Cook-Off. Back then,

barbecue cook-offs were a lot less cut-throat and a lot more fun.

Saturday morning, between my shifts at the judging table, I wandered around Murphy Park, expecting to meet a lot of earnest competitors. What I actually found was a bunch of unshaven, bleary-eyed guys snoozing on lawn chairs set up next to their smokers. Good thing it wasn't a beauty contest. It turns out that the real fun at a barbecue cook-off occurs the night before the judging. That's when the competitors stay up all night tending their fires and drinking too much beer.

Today, there is more money at stake for the winners and a new competitiveness fueled by reality television shows.

Television heroes like Myron Mixon encourage barbecue cook-off competitors to do anything to win. The results of this new attitude are both positive and negative.

On the downside, I don't judge barbecue cook-offs anymore. Mainly, that's because the meat submitted to the judges is now injected with potassium and other chemicals to aid moisture retention, doused with MSG to boost the flavor, and generally not anything I want to put in my mouth.

But on the positive side, Texas barbecue cook-off competitors have come up with some exciting new techniques for cooking ribs, chicken, and brisket that are easily adapted to the way we cook at home.

Then, as now, the cook-off competitors most willing to share their recipes are the ones who win the most trophies. That's because the secrets of prize-winning barbecue are patience, diligence, timing, the ability to judge cooking temperatures, and an instinct for what meat smells and feels like when it reaches the perfect level of doneness. Those secrets can't be stolen.

Harley's Pork Shoulder

I ASKED HARLEY TO GIVE ME A RECIPE FOR somebody who had never smoked meat before. "Tell 'em to start off with a pork shoulder. It's hard to mess up a pork shoulder," he said. Pork shoulder roast is also known as Boston butt.

1 bone-in pork shoulder roast (4 to 5 pounds)

6 tablespoons dry rub of your choice

2 onions, halved

4 cups mop sauce of your choice

Sandwich rolls, split, for serving

Barbecue sauce of your choice for serving

Season the pork roast with the dry rub, pressing the spice mix into the meat. Cover and refrigerate overnight.

The next day, set up your smoker for indirect heat with a water pan, and put the onions in the water pan. Use wood chips, chunks, or logs, and keep up a good level of smoke. Maintain a temperature between 210° and 250°F.

Place the roast in the smoker. Mop with the sauce every 30 minutes, turning the roast so it cooks evenly. The roast should be ready in 4 to 5 hours. The meat is done when it pulls easily away from the bone, but don't worry about overcooking it. It will just keep getting better. An internal temperature of around 170°F is good for sliced pork; aim for 200°F for pulled pork.

Slice or pull the pork from the bone, removing the big chunks of fat as you go. Shred the meat by hand and serve it on sandwich rolls with barbecue sauce.

SERVES 8 TO 10

Variation: Barbecued Leg of Lamb. Substitute a 3-pound bone-in leg of lamb for the pork shoulder. Serve with Mustard Sauce (page 109).

LEGENDS

Cook-Off Champion Harley Goerlitz

There are more than three hundred barbecue trophies in Harley Goerlitz's garage. He calls his team Harley's Fencing, which is also the name of his business. Harley has won eighteen first prizes in the Giddings Barbecue Cook-Off. (Giddings is his hometown.) He has also won the coveted Overall trophy at the Kansas City Royal, the Overall at the Taylor International, and First Place at the Brady Goat Cook-Off, and he was a runner-up at the Houston Rodeo and Livestock Show's cook-off. In short, Harley knows how to cook meat. So, one day during a competition, I asked him for some pointers for home barbecuers.

"First off, don't worry about buying a big, fancy smoker," he said. "You can make great barbecue in a Weber, if you know what you're doing." All around him, huge, fancy rigs worth thousands of dollars were billowing smoke. But Harley was cooking in a sawed-in-half oil drum.

Klassic Mop

THE KLASSIC KOOKERS BARBECUE TEAM OUT OF KILGORE, TEXAS, WAS competing in its fourteenth Houston Livestock Show and Rodeo Barbecue Cook-Off in 2001 when head cook Tommy Wimberly gave me the recipe for his mop. He keeps this mixture simmering in a five-gallon soup pot on the smoker whenever he barbecues, and he uses it on everything. You'll notice that Tommy keeps the proportions easy to handle—"I don't like measuring," he says. If necessary, you can cut down the amounts to fit the size of your soup pot.

One 16-ounce box brown sugar
One 32-ounce bottle Wesson oil
½ cup butter or margarine
One 17-ounce bottle distilled white vinegar
One 10-ounce bottle Worcestershire sauce
Large pinch of celery salt

1 head garlic, cloves separated, peeled, and crushed
4 or 5 onions, cut into large pieces
4 or 5 lemons, halved

Combine all of the ingredients in a large soup pot and add water to fill the pot nearly full. If your barbecue smoker has a firebox, set the pot on top of it and bring the contents to a simmer, stirring until the sugar dissolves, then keep the mop at a simmer. If it doesn't have a firebox, bring the mop to a simmer on the stove top. As the meat cooks, baste it with the mixture: Tommy uses a cotton mop, but a silicone brush is fine, too. If you start to run out of liquid near the end of your barbecuing, just add a little water to what's left in the pot.

MAKES ABOUT 8 QUARTS

MOPS *A mop is a basting sauce. In the old days, when forequarter and other large beef cuts were barbecued, mops were essential because the beef came out dry without them. Walter Jetton recommended that beginners use a basic basting liquid of cooking oil with a little seasoning added for beef. The idea was to try to replace the natural fat. (Jetton himself favored more elaborate basting sauces; see his recipe, Jetton's Beef Stock Mop, on page 165.)*

Brisket, the cut of choice for many barbecuers nowadays, doesn't really require any basting, since it is barbecued with much of the fat cap still on it. But cook-off competitors baste it anyway for added flavor (see chapter 11 for several brisket mops).

Award-winning cook-off competitors also baste poultry during the cooking process. Italian dressing, straight out of the bottle, is a popular dual-purpose marinade and mop for chicken. To avoid bacterial contamination, it is best to discard the marinade liquid and use fresh Italian dressing for the mop.

Pork cuts typically have plenty of fat, so pork mops don't need oil in them, but pork barbecuers swear by vinegar. A vinegar mop, they say, aids the tenderizing process. For a simple pork mop, you can use straight vinegar or add some crushed garlic cloves. Or you can adapt another mop recipe by adding more vinegar.

Most barbecue competitors have developed their own mop recipes that elaborate on these principles. Harley Goerlitz uses a basic mop during most of the cooking process, but adds a stick of butter to what's left of the mop toward the end to intensify the flavor.

Rockney Terry

Rockney Terry and his Falls County "Go Texan" team had entered the state's biggest shootout, the Houston Livestock Show and Rodeo Barbecue Cook-Off, more than a dozen times when I first caught up with them. The team won the Overall trophy at the rodeo cook-off in 1996 and the Chicken category in 1992.

Rockney Terry's Pork Rub

HERE'S AN EASY PORK RUB TO GET YOU STARTED on blending your own combinations.

¼ cup salt

¼ cup paprika

2 tablespoons sugar

2 tablespoons garlic powder

2 tablespoons onion powder

3 tablespoons cayenne pepper

2 tablespoons ground black pepper

Combine all of the ingredients in a bowl and mix well, then transfer to a shaker jar. The rub will keep in an airtight jar at room temperature for a couple of months.

MAKES ABOUT 1¼ CUPS

Heath Ray's Rub

HEATH RAY IS THE COMPETITION PITMASTER of the Cold River Cattle Company Barbecue Team, a perennial favorite at the Houston Livestock Show and Rodeo Barbecue Cook-Off. Ray uses this great all-around rub on briskets.

¾ cup kosher salt

½ cup coarsely ground black pepper

1 tablespoon cayenne pepper

2 tablespoons granulated garlic

2 tablespoons chili powder

Combine all of the ingredients in a bowl and mix well, then transfer to a shaker jar. The rub will keep in an airtight jar at room temperature for up to 1 month.

MAKES ABOUT 1½ CUPS

RUBS *The simplest dry rubs are nothing but salt and pepper—half and half is the usual ratio. The old meat markets add a touch of cayenne, too. Barbecue cook-off competitors generally favor rubs that also include garlic powder, ground dried chiles, and other spices.*

Harley Goerlitz and many other cook-off competitors market their own lines of barbecue seasoning blends. There are also many commercial dry rubs and seasoning mixes available in grocery and gourmet stores. (See page 288 for mail-order information.)

Tommy Wimberly, the head cook of the Klassic Kookers team from Kilgore, likes Tony Chachere's Original Creole Seasoning with some Adams Malabar black pepper added. Rockney Terry of the Falls County Barbecue Team uses barbecue rubs made by Adams Extract.

So, how do you pick a rub? First, you have to decide on the MSG issue. There's no doubt that MSG enhances the flavor of meat, but it gives some people a headache.

Next, check the ingredients list. For beef, you probably want plenty of salt, garlic powder, and pepper. If you're cooking chicken, you'll also want herbs. A pork rub, on the other hand, might have more sugar and paprika in it. You can buy a rub designed for almost any meat, but after a while you'll find yourself blending your own rubs. It's certainly a lot cheaper that way.

Sprinkle the rub generously over the surface of the meat. Then rub it in and allow the meat to absorb the flavor for a while. If possible, marinate the meat overnight in the refrigerator.

Try one or both of the rubs in this chapter for starters, then check out more rub recipes in the chapters that follow.

Rockney Terry's Brined Chicken

ROCKNEY TERRY'S SECRET TO GREAT BARBECUED CHICKEN—AND ONE REASON why he won the Chicken trophy in 1992—is brining. That single step saturates the bird with flavor and keeps it juicier during cooking.

2 quarts hot water

½ cup sea salt

2 tablespoons hot-pepper sauce

1 tablespoon freshly ground black pepper

1 tablespoon poultry seasoning

One 12-ounce can beer

1 whole fryer chicken (3 to 4 pounds)

¼ cup dry rub of your choice

3 cups Wish-Bone Italian dressing

In a large bowl or crock that will fit in your refrigerator, combine the water, salt, hot-pepper sauce, pepper, and poultry seasoning and stir until the salt dissolves. Add the beer, stir well, and then refrigerate until cold.

Remove the giblets from the chicken and reserve for another use. Turn the chicken breast-side down and, using a sharp knife or poultry shears, cut along the length of the backbone. Turn the chicken breast-side up and press against the breastbone to flatten it. Put the chicken in the brine and place a weight on top of it to keep it submerged. Refrigerate for 24 hours to cure.

Set up your smoker for indirect heat with a water pan. Use wood chips, chunks, or logs, and keep up a good level of smoke. Maintain a temperature between 225° and 275°F.

Remove the chicken from the brine and discard the brine. Pat the chicken dry, then sprinkle it all over with the rub and press the rub into the skin and meat. Lay the chicken, bone-side down, in the smoker and cook, mopping it with Italian dressing every 30 minutes, for about 3 hours, or until a thermometer inserted into the breast away from the bone registers 165°F. Alternatively, insert a knife tip into the thickest part of a thigh; if the juices run clear, the chicken is done. Serve immediately.

SERVES 2 TO 4

BRINING *Brining and curing are old meat-market techniques for improving the flavor of smoked meats. What we call* Canadian bacon *is actually a cold-smoked brined pork loin. At the City Market in Schulenburg, the staff makes a dried pork loin at Christmastime by injecting the pork with sweet bacon cure and then hot-smoking it until it shrinks.*

The barbecue cook-off teams that consistently win top honors always marinate or brine their chickens or pork loins before cooking. Brining is easy to do, and it makes a huge difference in the juiciness of the meat.

Barbecued Honey Pork Loin

A SWEETENER IS THE MAGIC INGREDIENT IN A PORK BRINE. HERE, HONEY IS used, but you can experiment with others sweet flavors as well, such as maple syrup or apple juice and brown sugar (see variations, following). Cooking a pork loin is different from cooking a pork shoulder, says Rockney Terry. Pork shoulder keeps getting better the longer it is cooked, but pork loin should be cooked just until it's done and then quickly removed from the heat before it dries out.

Serve with German Sweet Potato Salad (variation, page 127) and Leon O'Neal's Turnip Greens (page 154). This tastes great without barbecue sauce or with a mustard-based sauce such as Mustard Sauce (page 109).

2 quarts hot water
½ cup sea salt
¾ cup honey
2 tablespoons Tabasco sauce
1 tablespoon ground black pepper

1 boneless pork loin (4 to 6 pounds)
1¼ cups Rockney Terry's Pork Rub
  (page 76)
3 garlic cloves, minced

In a large bowl or crock that will fit in your refrigerator, combine the water, salt, honey, Tabasco, and pepper and stir until the salt dissolves. Refrigerate until cold.

Put the pork loin in the brine and place a weight on top of it to keep it submerged. Refrigerate for 36 to 48 hours to cure. To test if it is properly cured, slice off a little piece and fry it. If it is overcured, it will taste salty, and if it is undercured, it won't have a lot of flavor.

Set up your smoker for indirect heat with a water pan. Use wood chips, chunks, or logs, and keep up a good level of smoke. Maintain a temperature between 275° and 325°F.

Remove the pork from the brine and discard the brine. Pat the pork dry, then sprinkle it all over with the rub and the garlic and press them into the meat. Put the pork in the smoker and cook, turning it as needed to cook evenly, for about 3 hours, or until a thermometer inserted into the thickest part registers 145°F. Transfer the pork to a cutting board, cover it lightly with foil, and let it rest for 15 minutes before carving and serving.

SERVES 10

Variations:
Barbecued Maple Pork Loin. Replace the honey with 1 cup maple syrup.
Barbecued Apple Juice Pork Loin. Replace the honey and 1½ cups of the water with 2 cups apple juice and ¼ cup firmly packed brown sugar.

Marvin Lange

Marvin Lange of Thrall is the patriarch of the Lange family and the head cook of the Smokehouse Cookers barbecue team. The family team specializes in barbecued chicken.

Marvin Lange's Barbecued Chicken

WISH-BONE ITALIAN DRESSING IS THE FAVORITE marinade of Marvin Lange's Smokehouse Cookers barbecue team. They have won so many trophies for chicken at various Texas cook-offs that it's hard to argue with the decision to go with Wish-Bone. The chicken is marinated overnight in the dressing.

1 whole fryer chicken (about 3½ pounds)

¼ cup dry rub of your choice

6 cups Wish-Bone Italian dressing

Remove the giblets from the chicken and reserve for another use. Turn the chicken breast-side down and, using a sharp knife or poultry shears, cut along the length of the backbone. Turn the chicken breast-side up and press against the breastbone to flatten it. Sprinkle the chicken all over with the rub and press the rub into the skin and meat. Let the bird sit at room temperature for an hour or so. Put the chicken in a large resealable plastic bag, add 3 cups of the Italian dressing, seal the bag closed, and refrigerate overnight.

Set up your smoker for indirect heat with a water pan. Use wood chips, chunks, or logs, and keep up a good level of smoke. Maintain a temperature between 225° and 275°F.

Remove the chicken from the bag and discard the marinade. Lay the chicken, bone-side down, in the smoker and cook, mopping it with the remaining 3 cups Italian dressing every hour, for about 3 hours, or until a thermometer inserted into the breast away from the bone registers 165°F. Alternatively, insert a knife tip into the thickest part of a thigh; if the juices run clear, the chicken is done. Serve immediately.

SERVES 2 TO 4

Buttery Glazed Half Chicken

IN THE REST OF THE COUNTRY, COMPETITORS submit any six pieces of chicken for the chicken category, observes Ernest Servantes. Six breasts, six thighs, whatever they want. Myron Mixon smoke-braises boneless thighs in a muffin tin for his chicken entries. Other folks smoke drumsticks. A lot of competitors pull the skin off the chicken, scrape off all the fat, and stick the skin back on with toothpicks in order to get a chicken skin that is crispy instead of rubbery. But in Texas, the rules call for a half chicken, so there's a lot less manipulation.

Chicken is delicate and absorbs more smoky flavor than most other meats, so it is easy to overdo the smoking. It's also easy to burn the skin. That's why cook-off competitors often put the chicken in an aluminum pan for part of the cooking time.

4 to 6 half chickens
Buttery Chicken Injection
    (page 83)
Red River Ranch Chicken Rub
    (page 84)

4 to 6 tablespoons
    margarine or butter
Orange-Tiger Chicken Glaze
    (page 85)

Several hours before the chicken halves are scheduled to go in the smoker, inject them as directed on page 83 and then sprinkle each chicken half all over with the dry rub and press the rub into the skin and meat. Rub the outside of the chicken with any leftover marinade to help the dry rub stick to the skin. Refrigerate the chickens until it is time to prepare the smoker.

continued . . .

continued . . .

LEGENDS

Ernest Servantes

Pitmaster Ernest Servantes and his Burnt Bean Co. cook-off team have won dozens of barbecue cook-offs including the Grand Champion award in the Lone Star Barbecue Society's Cooker of the Year (COTY) contest in 2013 and 2014. He also won the Grill Masters version of the television show *Chopped*. He teaches a class called Master the Grill—BBQ Cooking School for aspiring cook-off competitors. Here's what he has to say about what's new in Texas barbecue cook-offs.

"The cooking techniques at Texas barbecue cook-offs have changed a lot in the last fifteen years. I think we are more influenced by cooking styles in other parts of the country than we used to be. Maybe it's because of all the television shows; maybe it's the cookbooks.

"Texas barbecue judges are looking for sweet-flavored glazes on ribs and chicken now. At home, I like spicy ribs and simple smoked chicken, but you can't cook that at a competition. Dry rub ribs aren't winning, and nobody is winning the Chicken category with Italian dressing marinades anymore."

Prepare a smoker with lump hardwood charcoal and a water pan and maintain a temperature between 275° and 300°F. This is an excellent recipe for orange, peach, or apple wood, if you have any; otherwise, a little post oak or hickory wood will do. You want a little smoke, but not too much. Melt about 2 tablespoons margarine in each of two or three half-sheet-size aluminum foil pans (use two pans for four chicken halves and three pans for six chicken halves). Mix a little dry rub into the butter in each pan, then place two chicken halves in each pan.

Place the pans in the smoker and cook for 1 hour. Then, wearing fireproof gloves so as not to tear the chicken skin, carefully transfer each chicken half to the grate and continue smoking for another 30 minutes at 250°F, rotating the birds as needed for even cooking. Using a thermometer, begin checking the internal temperature of the chicken, and continue cooking until it registers 160°F. Return the chicken halves to the aluminum pans and begin painting them with the glaze. The chicken is done when the breast registers 165°F and the thigh registers 175°F. Serve immediately.

MAKES 4 TO 6 HALF CHICKEN PORTIONS

Buttery Chicken Injection

THE FIRST PROBLEM IS FINDING A GOOD CHICKEN. You can't use "enhanced" chicken (see page 84) in a competition.

Instead of marinating or brining, winning teams are injecting their chickens. There are all sorts of injection ingredients—butter, chicken stock, you name it. You have to work real slow or all of the liquid just shoots back out of the hole when you pull out the needle.

Recipes that call for garlic powder, black pepper, and other spices that do not completely dissolve won't work for an injection. The particles get caught in the injector. That's why you want to cook your injection sauce in a saucepan on the stove top to dissolve the ingredients completely before you load the injector. You can avoid garlic powder by simmering the sauce with garlic cloves and then straining it.

½ cup salted butter

2 tablespoons apple juice

2 tablespoons chicken stock

1 teaspoon Worcestershire sauce

1 teaspoon Tabasco, or to taste

1 teaspoon cane syrup or molasses

½ teaspoon salt, or to taste

3 garlic cloves, crushed

In a small saucepan, combine all of the ingredients over medium heat, bring to a simmer, and simmer for 5 minutes, making sure that the salt and cane syrup are completely dissolved. Remove from the heat, strain through a fine-mesh sieve, and then let cool for a minute or two, but not so long that the butter begins to solidify.

Fill a flavor injector with the marinade and insert the needle into the exposed meat at various locations, pushing it well into the chicken. Don't puncture the skin. Inject the liquid slowly and evenly until you feel pressure, then slowly pull out the needle. If you push too hard or pull out the needle too fast, the liquid will squirt out of the chicken.

MAKES ENOUGH FOR 6 HALF CHICKENS

LEGENDS

Mickey Speaker on Chicken

Mickey Speaker and his Hard Heads BBQ Team have been competing in barbecue cook-offs for over thirty years, specializing in the Chicken category. Speaker does the barbecue chicken cooking demonstrations at Barbecue Summer Camp (see page 48).

"In the old days, we marinated our chickens, but now we inject them—like everybody else," he told me while cooking half a dozen birds. Speaker's team uses Ritter's Chicken Injection Marinade, a popular commercial product that comes in powdered form. You mix the powder with your choice of water, apple juice, or chicken stock and inject the chickens several hours before cooking. Ritter's also sells a variety of rubs, including the popular Cluckin Buckin Rub.

"We are working on our own injection and rub recipes," Speaker told me.

Enhanced Meats

The term *enhanced* is the meat industry's euphemism for products that have been injected with potassium and salted water. The injections make the meat juicy, but they also add about 15 percent in water weight, which increases industry profits. Chicken and pork are the most frequently enhanced meats.

Marinating, brining, or injecting an enhanced meat product is a waste of time. The meat is already so saturated with chemicals and salted water that it can't absorb any more liquid.

Red River Ranch Chicken Rub

THE COMBINATION OF RANCH DRESSING MIX and sweet Hungarian paprika results in a red rub that makes chicken skin look great.

½ cup sweet Hungarian paprika
¼ cup sugar
¼ cup garlic salt
2 tablespoons powdered ranch dressing mix

1 teaspoon poultry seasoning
1 teaspoon ground white pepper
½ teaspoon cayenne pepper

Combine all of the ingredients in a spice grinder and process until well blended. Do not reduce the mixture to a fine powder. The rub will keep in an airtight jar at room temperature for up to 1 month.

MAKES ENOUGH FOR 6 HALF CHICKENS

Orange-Tiger Chicken Glaze

TIGER SAUCE IS A MILD, SWEET-AND-SOUR cayenne sauce from Reily Foods in New Orleans. Because it has a mellow chile flavor without a lot of heat, it has become a favorite of barbecue competitors who don't want to overwhelm the judges' taste buds. If you like your chicken spicy, substitute a hotter pepper sauce, like Sriracha, Frank's RedHot, Texas Pete, or Tabasco.

One 18-ounce jar orange
    marmalade
⅓ cup Tiger Sauce
⅓ cup honey
⅓ cup firmly packed
    brown sugar

In a small saucepan, combine all of the ingredients over medium heat and cook, stirring constantly, until the sugar is completely dissolved. Remove from the heat and pass the glaze through a sieve to remove the orange peel. Alternatively, if you would like the deliciously bitter flavor of the peel in your chicken rub, transfer the glaze to a blender and purée until smooth.

Use immediately, or transfer to an airtight jar and store in the refrigerator for up to 2 weeks.

MAKES ABOUT 1½ CUPS

Favorite Glazes

Ernest Servantes glazes his competition ribs with jalapeño jelly, but you can use any kind of jelly thinned with a little hot butter. Paint it on thick and shiny like a coat of shellac. Servantes says that the guys who are winning these days are using glazes like Daigle's Cajun Sweet & Sour Sauce or Craig Sherry's Texas Rib Candy (see Online and Mail-Order Sources, page 288).

Johnny Trigg

Born in 1938, Johnny Trigg graduated from North Texas State University and then spent most of his life in the insurance industry. He started entering barbecue competitions in 1990, and the cook-off circuit became his retirement hobby.

He and his Smokin' Triggers team won the Grand Champion title at the Jack Daniel's World Championship Invitational Barbecue in Lynchburg, Tennessee, in 2000 and 2003. He appeared several times on *BBQ Pitmasters*, winning the television show's Grand Champion title in season three.

Johnny Trigg has some sage advice for backyard barbecuers: Use lump charcoal, not briquettes, which contain fillers. And throw away your old spices every six months and buy some fresh stuff.

Johnny Trigg's Spareribs

JOHNNY TRIGG'S RIB WRAP IS SHEER GENIUS. HE spreads margarine, brown sugar, hot-pepper sauce, and honey on aluminum foil in the shape of the rack of ribs, and then lays the rack, meat-side down, on the mixture, wraps the foil around the rack, and returns the ribs to the smoker.

Trigg starts with what he calls "squeeze butter" (actually Parkay Squeeze). Although squeezable margarine may be the secret ingredient of winning competitors, feel free to substitute softened butter.

Don't bother to measure the ingredients precisely, as the bigger the rack of ribs, the more margarine, brown sugar, and honey you will need. What's important is to cover a large enough area of the foil to coat the whole rack. Don't try this recipe with the water-injected "enhanced" pork ribs sold at most grocery stores—you will end up with a foil package full of water.

1 rack 4 and up pork spareribs (5 to 6 pounds)
1 cup dry rub of your choice
¼ to ½ cup squeezable margarine or softened butter
¼ to ½ cup firmly packed brown sugar

1 teaspoon hot-pepper sauce, or to taste
¼ to ½ cup honey
About 1½ cups barbecue sauce or glaze of your choice

Trim the rib rack St. Louis style and remove the membrane (see page 197). Sprinkle the meat side of the ribs with the dry rub, pressing it into the meat, and let the rack sit at room temperature for around 45 minutes.

Set up your smoker for indirect heat with a water pan. Use wood chips, chunks, or logs, and keep up a good level of smoke. Maintain a temperature between 225° and 275°F. Cut a piece of heavy-duty aluminum foil large enough to wrap the ribs completely. Spread the margarine over an area of the foil the size of the rib rack. Sprinkle the margarine with the brown sugar and pepper sauce, then drizzle the honey evenly over the top. Lay the rack, meat-side down, on the margarine mixture and wrap the foil around the rack, sealing the packet tightly closed.

Place the ribs in the smoker and cook between 225° and 275°F for 3 hours. Remove the packet from the cooker and discard the foil. Coat the meat side of the rack with the barbecue sauce, return the rack, unwrapped and meat-side up, to the smoker, and cook at 225°F for about 1 hour, or until the ribs are done. To test if the ribs are ready, using tongs, pick up one end of the rack, and if the rack is just about to break, the ribs are done. Be careful that they do not burn.

Remove the rack from the cooker and immediately apply more barbecue sauce. Carve between the bones into individual ribs (Trigg uses an electric knife), pile the ribs on a platter, and serve.

SERVES 3 TO 4

Variation:
Home Version. Cook-off competitors have to do all their cooking on the barbecue pit, but home cooks have the freedom to employ modern conveniences. If you start Johnny Trigg's Spareribs in an oven set at 250°F for 3 hours, then put them on the smoker after you unwrap the aluminum foil and proceed as directed with the glazing, you will have exactly the same results. Be sure to put the foil-wrapped packages in a roasting pan before you put them in the oven—if you puncture the foil while handling, the juices will leak all over the oven.

Robert Sierra

Known for their elaborate
and ornate barbecue trailers,
Robert Sierra and his S&S
Pit Crew are one of the top
barbecue cook-off teams in
Texas. "We've been cooking
for ten years," Sierra told me.
"We've been on the Travel
Channel and on lots of other
television shows, including
All You Can Meat."

The team has won trophies
in four states, but none of
those victories was sweeter
than the Grand Champion
title at the twentieth annual
Juneteenth Barbecue Cook-
Off in Sierra's hometown of
San Marcos. Robert Sierra
and the organizers dedicated
the event to an old friend,
neighbor, and cook-off
regular named Billy Waters,
of Billy's Southern Q, who
had just passed away. "I think
we did him proud this week
dedicating this hometown
cook-off in his honor," Sierra
said. The team also cooks at
the Peace Officers' Memorial
Foundation Cookoff, an event
that benefits the families
of fallen peace officers.

Robert Sierra's
Baby Back Ribs

"THE NEW, THICKER BABY BACK RIBS ARE CUT
with more loin on top, so they take longer to cook,"
Robert Sierra explains. "I like to slather some mustard on the meat and season it heavy. Then I like
to cook it low and slow with oak wood. I usually layer
my rub—after the mustard—starting with the salt,
then the black pepper, garlic powder, onion powder,
and finally the brown sugar."

2 racks baby back ribs
   (about 3½ pounds each)
1 cup yellow mustard
½ cup kosher salt
¼ cup ground black pepper
2 tablespoons garlic powder
1 tablespoon onion powder

½ cup firmly packed
   brown sugar
About 1½ cups glaze of
   your choice (see Favorite
   Glazes, page 85; optional)

Place the ribs, meat-side up, on a work surface. Spread them with the mustard, and then sprinkle them with the salt, pepper, garlic powder, onion powder, and brown sugar. Press the spices and sugar into the wet mustard to form a coating. Let dry at room temperature for 20 to 30 minutes or until the spices are set.

Prepare a smoker with oak wood and a water pan and maintain a very low temperature of around 225°F. Put the ribs, bone-side down, in the smoker for 3 hours. Flip the ribs so they are meat-side down, being careful not to knock off the spice mixture, and cook for 1 hour. Remove the ribs from the smoker, wrap them in heavy-duty aluminum foil, return them to the smoker, and cook for 1 hour longer.

Remove the foil packet from the smoker, discard the foil, and apply the glaze to the meat side of each rack, if desired. Return the racks, meat-side up, to the smoker and cook for 1 hour longer, or until tender. To test if the ribs are ready, using tongs, pick up one end of the rack, and if the rack is just about to break, the ribs are done.

Carve between each rib and serve fanned on a platter.

SERVES 4 TO 6

Sierra is a leading light of the "yellow mustard school." Whether he is cooking brisket or ribs, he always starts his marinating process with a layer of French's mustard, which helps the spices stick to the meat and form a thick bark. "Some people prefer to wet the meat with pickle juice, but French's mustard works better, if you ask me," says Sierra.

THE BATTLE OVER SAUCE

Disappearing Traditions
versus Modern Tastes

Stirring barbecue gravy in cast-iron washpots at the Annual Millheim Father's Day Barbecue.
Photo by Robert Lerma

arbecue sauce wasn't served in the old meat markets of Central Texas. Salt, pepper, and post oak smoke were the only things that touched the meat. "That's the way it's been done for over a hundred years," says Rick Schmidt, of Kreuz Market in Lockhart. Kreuz Market never served side dishes either.

Kreuz Market moved from its original location in downtown Lockhart to a new building in 1999. Rick retired in 2011 and turned the business over to his son Keith. Keith Schmidt added pork ribs, brisket, beans, German potato salad, and sauerkraut to the menu—but there still isn't any sauce.

"We feel that sauce is for covering up the flavor of the meat, which we want to accent, so we have no sauce," Keith explains.

But the Schmidts aren't the only barbecuers with strong opinions in Texas. Other barbecue proponents always use sauce, and they don't put much stock in the methods of Central Texas meat markets. That's not barbecuing; that's just smoking, say the owners of Cooper's, one of the state's most famous outlets of cowboy barbecue.

Arguments over cooking methods, the right kind of wood, the correct design of a smoker, and whether or not to use barbecue sauce have raged in Texas for as long as anyone can remember. It's partly because Texans like to argue. And it's partly because Texas barbecue is an amalgamation of several formerly distinct styles that haven't entirely reconciled with one another.

Each of these barbecue styles once had its own rules. In East Texas, as in most of the Old South, pork was the most common meat and open pits were favored. The woods used for smoking were red oak, hickory, and its cousin, pecan. In Mexican and West Texas barbecue, where goat and later beef were the favorites, mesquite was the wood of choice, and meats were cooked directly over the coals. German meat markets became famous for serving smoked sausages and other meats on butcher paper without sides or sauces. But the distinctions among the styles are slowly being lost.

"We started serving barbecue sauce in the early 1980s, but we only gave it to people who asked for it," says Edgar Black Jr. of Black's in Lockhart. Black's father started his meat market and barbecue in 1932, serving smoked beef and sausage rings on butcher paper with nothing on the side but crackers. But by the early 1980s, it had become too hard to explain the unusual history of meat-market barbecue to all of the people who

were coming to Texas from other places, Edgar Black Jr. says. They wanted potato salad, they wanted beans, they wanted sauce. Black's finally gave in.

The majority of Texas barbecue joints now serve a little bit of everything. You'll always find some kind of beef offered and usually a German-style sausage along with Southern-style pork with barbecue sauce, Mexican tortillas, West Texas beans, and sides from all over the place—not to mention banana pudding, coconut cake, and sweet potato pie. Some places try to maintain a degree of stylistic purity, but few succeed.

That's why when you say "Texas barbecue," no one can be entirely sure what you are talking about. East Texas pork ribs slow-smoked over pecan wood? Elgin hot guts? Cowboy beef brisket cooked over mesquite? Brownsville barbacoa? It may sound as though we're confused, but there's another way to look at it.

The best way to preserve our traditions is to constantly disagree about what Texas barbecue really is. As long as there's some disagreement, the distinctions are kept alive.

The sauces in this chapter represent the different points of view about barbecue sauce in the state—except for the point of view that insists you should use no sauce at all.

The interior of Louie Mueller
Barbecue in Taylor.
Photo by Wyatt McSpadden

Barbecue Joint Brisket Sauce

THE BEST BARBECUE SAUCES IN TEXAS ALL SHARE A SECRET INGREDIENT. A rare chile? An exotic herb? An unexpected spice? No, the secret is meat drippings. Brisket drippings are what make the sauce so good at Cooper's in Llano, the cowboy barbecue joint that's George W. Bush's favorite. Lots of other places I have visited use the same technique.

"You collect all the juices that flow out of the meat while you're slicing and add them back to the sauce. Just like you're making a good gravy," Ray Esquivel at Ray's Roundup and QuickStop outside of Falfurrias told me as he sliced a juicy brisket. (Ray's Roundup isn't open anymore, but Ray's sage advice lives on.)

You can't save barbecue sauce that has meat drippings in it, as it goes bad quickly. The trick is to make up a big batch of basic sauce and keep it in the refrigerator. Then you heat up what you need and add the meat drippings just before serving. It's a good trick for improving bottled sauces, too.

2 cups Ancho Barbecue Sauce (facing page) or the sauce of your choice

Up to 1 cup meat drippings

Just before serving your barbecue, heat the barbecue sauce and add fresh meat drippings as you slice your barbecue. Serve all of the sauce the day you make it, as it does not keep well.

MAKES ABOUT 3 CUPS

Ancho Barbecue Sauce

USE THIS AS A BASIC BARBECUE SAUCE, ADDING MEAT JUICES AND CUT-UP meat scraps left over from carving just before serving.

3 ancho chiles, stemmed and seeded

1 tablespoon olive oil

2 cups diced onion

7 garlic cloves, minced

1 cup ketchup

½ cup Worcestershire sauce

⅓ cup firmly packed brown sugar

¼ cup cider vinegar

¼ cup fresh lemon juice

1½ tablespoons prepared mustard

Kosher salt

Soak the chiles in hot water to cover for 30 minutes, or until soft. Drain and set aside.

In a heavy saucepan, heat the olive oil over medium heat. Add the onion and garlic and sauté for 3 minutes, or until they begin to wilt. Add the ketchup and anchos and sauté for 4 minutes. Add the Worcestershire, brown sugar, vinegar, lemon juice, mustard, and 2 teaspoons salt; stir well; and simmer gently, stirring frequently, for 30 to 40 minutes, or until slightly thickened.

Remove from the heat, taste and adjust the seasoning with salt if needed, and let cool. Transfer to a blender or food processor and purée until smooth. The sauce will keep in an airtight container in the refrigerator for up to 3 weeks. Reheat before serving.

MAKES ABOUT 4 CUPS

Cattlemen conversing after lunch at the San Angelo Livestock Show, 1939. *Photo by Russell Lee*

Spicy Chipotle Sauce

THE ALWAYS POPULAR FLAVOR OF CHIPOTLE CHILES ADDS A PLEASANT dimension to smoky barbecue sauces.

One 7-ounce can chipotle chiles in
  adobo sauce
2 tablespoons butter
1 cup minced onion
4 garlic cloves, minced
3 cups ketchup
1 cup water

1 cup orange juice
1 cup cider vinegar
¼ cup molasses or cane syrup
1½ cups firmly packed light brown sugar
1 tablespoon Worcestershire sauce
1 tablespoon kosher salt

Seed the chiles, then transfer them to a blender along with the sauce from the can and purée until smooth. Set aside.

In a large saucepan, melt the butter over medium heat. Add the onion and sauté for about 5 minutes, or until it begins to soften. Add the garlic and continue to sauté for 5 minutes longer, or until the onion and garlic are soft. Add the puréed chiles, ketchup, water, orange juice, vinegar, molasses, brown sugar, Worcestershire, and salt and stir well. Bring to a simmer, stirring to dissolve the sugar, and cook gently for 15 minutes to blend the flavors.

Remove from the heat and let cool. The sauce will keep in an airtight container in the refrigerator for up to 3 weeks. Reheat before serving.

MAKES ABOUT 2 QUARTS

Luling Barbecue Sauce

FAMILY FEUDS ARE STILL BEING FOUGHT OVER THE FAMOUS BARBECUE sauce at City Market in Luling. Here's my version—in blind taste tests between the original and this copycat recipe, the copycat wins every time.

1 cup water
½ cup Louisiana hot sauce
½ cup yellow mustard
½ cup cider vinegar
¾ cup ketchup

¼ cup firmly packed brown sugar
1 tablespoon granulated sugar
2 teaspoons salt
1 tablespoon coarsely ground black pepper

In a small saucepan, combine all of the ingredients over medium heat and heat, stirring, until the sugars and salt have completely dissolved. Lower the heat to a gentle simmer and cook for a few minutes to blend the flavors.

Remove from the heat and let cool. The sauce will keep in an airtight container in the refrigerator for up to 1 month. Reheat before serving.

MAKES ABOUT 3½ CUPS

William Benedict "Bill" Smolik

SMOLIK'S MEATS & BBQ, CUERO

William Benedict "Bill" Smolik was a third-generation sausage maker and barbecue man. His grandfather, a Bohemian Czech, smoked sausage on the family farm near Hallettsville in the late 1800s. His father, William Harris Smolik, opened Smolik's Meat Market in Karnes City in 1918. Bill Smolik's son, Michael, took over the restaurant after Bill Smolik died in 2007. Michael and his wife Camille are carrying the Smolik barbecue tradition on to the fourth generation.

Easy Meat Market Sauce

BARBECUE SAUCE IS SERVED GRUDGINGLY BY some Central Texas meat markets. I got this recipe from Bill Smolik, who grew up cooking barbecue at his dad's place, the legendary Smolik's Meat Market in Karnes City, which was founded in 1928.

3 cups ketchup

2 cups water

Dash of Worcestershire
  sauce

Dash of vegetable oil

1 teaspoon salt

3 tablespoons brown sugar

1 teaspoon ground
  dried chile

In a saucepan, combine all of the ingredients over medium heat and heat, stirring, until the sugar has completely dissolved and the sauce begins to bubble.

Remove from the heat and let cool. The sauce will keep in an airtight container in the refrigerator for up to 3 weeks. Reheat before serving.

MAKES ABOUT 5 CUPS

Franklin's Espresso Barbecue Sauce

BEFORE HE STARTED COOKING BARBECUE FOR A LIVING, AARON FRANKLIN worked in a coffee house, and his original barbecue trailer was parked behind a friend's coffee-roasting operation. That's how Franklin came up with his espresso-flavored barbecue sauce. It tastes great with brisket, but it's good with Lockhart Prime Rib (page 242), too.

1½ cups ketchup

½ cup white vinegar

½ cup cider vinegar

¼ cup dark soy sauce

1 tablespoon garlic powder

1 tablespoon onion powder

¼ cup brown sugar

3 tablespoons freshly pulled espresso

Brisket drippings, for flavoring

Mix the ketchup, both vinegars, the soy sauce, garlic and onion powders, and sugar together in a saucepan and bring to a simmer over medium heat, stirring occasionally. Remove from the heat, stir in the espresso, then add brisket drippings to taste. Let cool, then transfer to a jar, bottle, squeeze bottle, or however you want to store it. Store in the refrigerator for up to 2 weeks.

MAKES ABOUT 2 CUPS

Rebekah's Grapefruit-Chipotle Sauce

I HAD THIS SOUTH TEXAS GRAPEFRUIT-CHIPOTLE SAUCE AT A BARBECUE on a ranch near Victoria. It pairs especially well with pork and brisket, but it's good with all kinds of barbecue.

One 7-ounce can chipotle chiles in adobo sauce

2 tablespoons butter

1 cup minced onion

4 garlic cloves, minced

1 cup fresh Rio Red grapefruit juice

1 cup cider vinegar

¼ cup molasses

1½ cups firmly packed brown sugar

3 cups ketchup

1 tablespoon Worcestershire sauce

1 cup water

1 tablespoon salt

Seed the chiles, then transfer them to a blender along with the sauce from the can and purée until smooth. Set aside.

In a small skillet, melt the butter over medium heat. Add the onion and sauté for about 5 minutes, or until it begins to soften. Add the garlic and continue to sauté for 5 minutes longer, or until the onion and garlic are soft. Add the puréed chiles, grapefruit juice, vinegar, molasses, brown sugar, ketchup, Worcestershire, water, and salt, stir well, and simmer for 15 minutes to blend the flavors.

Remove from the heat and let cool. The sauce will keep in an airtight container in the refrigerator for up to 3 weeks. Reheat before serving.

MAKES ABOUT 2 QUARTS

Lady Bird Johnson's Barbecue Sauce

BUTTER WAS A PRIME INGREDIENT IN OLD SOUTHERN-STYLE BARBECUE sauces. Mrs. Johnson used to send this recipe to people who wrote her at the White House.

4 tablespoons butter

¼ cup vinegar

¼ cup ketchup

¼ cup fresh lemon juice

¼ cup Worcestershire sauce

1 tablespoon minced garlic (optional)

Salt and ground black pepper

Tabasco sauce for seasoning

In a small saucepan, melt the butter over medium heat. Add the vinegar, ketchup, lemon juice, Worcestershire, and garlic (if using) and season with salt, pepper, and Tabasco. Bring to a boil, stirring often.

Remove from the heat and let cool. The sauce will keep in an airtight container in the refrigerator for up to 2 weeks. Reheat before serving.

MAKES ABOUT 1 CUP

Barbara Bush's Barbecue Sauce

IN THE GEORGE H. W. BUSH ERA, MARGARINE WAS BEING PROMOTED AS AN alternative to butter for health-conscious barbecue fans. During her White House years, Barbara Bush gave out a recipe card with barbecued chicken on one side and this barbecue sauce on the other.

2¼ cups water

¼ cup cider vinegar

¾ cup sugar

½ cup butter or margarine

⅓ cup yellow mustard

2 onions, coarsely chopped

½ teaspoon salt

½ teaspoon ground black pepper

2½ cups ketchup

½ cup Worcestershire sauce

6 to 8 tablespoons fresh lemon juice

Cayenne pepper for seasoning

In a large saucepan, combine the water, vinegar, sugar, butter, mustard, onions, salt, and black pepper over medium-high heat and bring to a boil, stirring to dissolve the sugar. Turn the heat to low and simmer for 20 minutes, or until the onions are tender. Add the ketchup, Worcestershire, and lemon juice to taste; season with cayenne; and simmer for 45 minutes longer to blend the flavors. Taste and adjust the seasoning.

Remove from the heat and let cool. The sauce will keep in an airtight container in the refrigerator for up to 3 weeks. Reheat before serving.

MAKES ABOUT 6 CUPS

Mustard Sauce

HARLEY GOERLITZ ONCE COMPETED IN THE LAMB DIVISION AT THE
American Royal Invitational in Kansas City, Missouri. Unlike Texas cook-offs,
where sauce is prohibited, at this event he was supposed to submit the meat
with sauce on the side. "I lost points for serving regular old red barbecue sauce,"
Harley said. "They told me barbecued lamb is supposed to be served with mustard
sauce. How was I supposed to know?"

Here's a mustard sauce for lamb, just in case you ever get into the finals.

½ cup Dijon mustard

½ cup apple juice

⅔ cup molasses

2 teaspoons salt

1 teaspoon crushed garlic

1 teaspoon ground black pepper

In a small saucepan, combine all of the ingredients over low heat and stir until
well combined and heated through.

Remove from the heat and let cool. The sauce will keep in an airtight container
in the refrigerator for up to 3 weeks. Reheat before serving.

MAKES ABOUT 2 CUPS

Shaker Bottle Pepper Sauce

IF YOU DON'T HAVE YOUR OWN PEQUÍN CHILE BUSH, YOU CAN SUBSTITUTE habaneros, serranos, or just about any other fresh hot chile in this recipe. In Jamaica, cooks make this sauce with Scotch bonnets and keep it in a pancake syrup dispenser. You can use the sauce for any recipe in this book that calls for hot-pepper sauce.

½ cup pequín or other fresh hot chiles

3 or 4 carrot slices (optional)

3 or 4 onion pieces (optional)

½ cup distilled white vinegar

If using pequín or other small chiles, clean a previously used pepper shaker bottle with boiling water. If using larger chiles, such as serranos or habaneros, double the other ingredients and use a pancake syrup dispenser. Pack the container with the chiles. Add the carrot and onion (if using).

In a small saucepan, heat the vinegar over low heat until it steams slightly. Pour the vinegar over the vegetables, submerging them completely. Let cool, cover, and let sit for 1 day before using.

You can use the vinegar as a hot-pepper sauce, or you can open the bottle to take out a few chiles as needed. The bottle can be refilled with vinegar about three times. The sauce will keep at room temperature for up to 6 months.

MAKES ONE 12-OUNCE BOTTLE

Chipotle Ketchup

IMPORTED MEXICAN BÚFALO BRAND CHIPOTLE SAUCE MAKES A GREAT RIB marinade (see Art Blondin's Chipotle-Marinated Ribs, page 204). If you can't find the Búfalo sauce in your grocery store, you can make your own chipotle ketchup. It's not only a great base for barbecue sauces, it's also remarkable on french fries, onion rings, and hamburgers.

3 dried chipotle peppers
   or 3 canned chipotle peppers
3 dried ancho chiles
3 dried guajillo or pasilla chiles
1 small white onion, diced
5 garlic cloves, minced

2 tablespoons packed brown sugar,
   or more to taste
2 tablespoons ground cumin
1 teaspoon dried Mexican oregano
2 cups tomato paste
Salt and ground black pepper

Remove the seeds and stems from all the chiles. Place all the chiles, the onion, and garlic in a large saucepan and cover with plenty of water. Bring to a boil over high heat, lower the heat, and simmer for about 15 minutes.

Remove the chiles, onion, and garlic from the pan with a slotted spoon and transfer to a food processor. Add the brown sugar, cumin, oregano, tomato paste, and a cup of the liquid the chiles were cooked in. Purée, adding more chile liquid until you reach the desired thickness. Adjust the seasonings with salt and pepper, and add more brown sugar if desired.

The ketchup will keep in an airtight container in the refrigerator for several months.

MAKES ABOUT 5 CUPS

Barbecued Tomato Salsa

AFTER YOU FINISH BARBECUING, HAVE YOU EVER STOOD THERE ADMIRING the leftover coals, thinking what a shame it is to waste them? Here's a sauce that lets you take advantage of those coals.

Smoking tomatoes is a great alternative to roasting them in the oven, and you can use them in all kinds of recipes. Here, they make an outstanding salsa that you can serve on barbacoa or lengua or with tortilla chips as an appetizer.

3 tomatoes, quartered

½ onion, sliced into rings

2 large jalapeño chiles

1 tablespoon chipotle purée

1 tablespoon lemon juice

½ cup chopped cilantro

Salt

Place the tomatoes, onion, and jalapeños on a hot grill, a good distance from the direct fire, and let them smoke for at least 15 minutes, turning several times. Remove as much skin as possible from the tomatoes and jalapeños. Halve the jalapeños and remove the seeds and stems. Transfer the tomatoes, onion, and jalapeños to a food processor. Add the chipotle purée and lemon juice and purée for 30 seconds, or just until chunky. Transfer to a bowl and add the cilantro. Season with salt. Serve immediately.

MAKES 2 TO 3 CUPS

Pico de Gallo

DOWN IN THE LOWER RIO GRANDE VALLEY, THEY USE THIS KIND OF fresh salsa for barbacoa and lengua tacos, or for any kind of smoked meat served on a tortilla.

5 jalapeño chiles, stems and seeds removed, minced
1 cup diced tomato
1 cup chopped onion
2 cups coarsely chopped cilantro leaves
1 tablespoon lemon juice
Salt and ground black pepper

In a bowl, combine the jalapeños, tomato, onion, and cilantro. Add the lemon juice, season with salt and pepper, and mix. Serve at once, or cover and hold in the refrigerator for a couple of days.

MAKES ABOUT 2 CUPS

BUTCHER PAPER FEASTS

The Old German
Meat Markets

Smoked meats, sausage ring, white bread, and crackers served on a sheet of butcher paper at Kreuz Market in Lockhart.
Photo by Wyatt McSpadden

If you follow your nose from Taylor down to Elgin, from Elgin out to La Grange, and south through small towns like Luling, Weimar, and Hallettsville, you'll find a bunch of smoky old meat markets with German and Czech names where butchers still sell fresh chops and roasts in front and barbecue in the back. This unique style of barbecue traces its origins to the state's German and Czech settlers.

The rest of the world thinks that all Texas pioneers were cowboys. In truth, some of the fathers of the Lone Star State were political and philosophical radicals who came here from Germany and Bohemia to live on communes. The legacy of our eccentric Bohemian forefathers lives on in such quirky places as Luckenbach, Shiner, and South Austin.

Johann Friedrich Ernst was the original German pioneer in Texas. In 1831, Ernst received a land grant of more than four thousand acres in present-day Austin County. The excited Ernst wrote letters to friends back home describing an earthly paradise of abundant fish and game, mild weather, and easy farming. This set off a steady stream of German immigration to Texas that continued for the next fifty years.

Some of the German settlers were middle-class farm folk hungry for land. Others were freethinkers whose lofty ideals were suppressed by restrictive religious dogma in Germany.

The Forty, for example, was a group of college students—followers of socialist visionaries like Fourier and Cabet—who formed a utopian society in Germany. They sailed across the Atlantic to live out their dreams, and in 1847 they founded the communal settlement of Bettina on the Llano River, basing it on the principles of "friendship, freedom, and equality." The group included two musicians, an engineer, a theologian, an agriculturist, two architects, seven lawyers, four foresters, and an army lieutenant. Unfortunately, the community was long on intellectuals and short on butchers and bakers. In less than a year, the settlement collapsed due to incessant arguments over kitchen duties. When the commune broke up, some of these young communists moved to Austin and became founding fathers of Texas. Others stayed in the Hill Country and became the patriarchs of free-thinking political and philosophical dynasties.

In the 1840s, a group of German noblemen took their fellow citizens to Texas by the thousands with the idea of founding a German colony. These settlers, and more who followed after the Civil War, created the Texas "German belt," a large swath of German farm communities dotting the countryside from Houston to the Hill Country. By 1850, Germans made up 5 percent of the state's population.

By the 1890s, when the German belt was at its peak, a large area of Texas had developed the patterns of Teutonic civilization. In villages of half-timbered houses and Gothic churches, German-speaking Texans drank Bohemian-style beers like Shiner Bock and ate smoked sausage and sauerkraut.

German butchers smoked pork loins and sausages, just as they had done in Germany. Their regular customers took the artisanal sausages and smoked pork home and served it with the traditional German accompaniments. To a casual observer (especially a hungry one), the differences between these German smoked meats and Southern barbecue were subtle.

Itinerant farmworkers who came through town during the harvest bought the smoked meats at butcher shops and ate them on the spot. Side dishes were what they could find on the store's shelves—usually just crackers and pickles. Thus began the meat-market barbecue tradition.

Some of the most famous barbecue joints in Texas, like City Market in Luling and Kreuz Market and Smitty's in Lockhart, are still butcher shops. They never did become restaurants.

To this day, they offer barbecue the way the farmworkers ate it—with no plates, no knives, and no forks—just a slab of smoked meat on a piece of butcher paper.

Many other meat markets have made concessions to the popular concept of barbecue and offer utensils, plates, and side orders. A few holdouts, like Kreuz Market and Smitty's, still refuse to serve barbecue sauce. Great smoked meats don't need sauces, Kreuz proprietor Rick Schmidt will tell you. And once you've eaten Kreuz's smoked prime rib, smoked pork loin, and smoked sausage links, you tend to agree with him.

Meat market barbecue is cooked and seasoned differently from Southern barbecue, too. In East Texas, pork is often rubbed with a spice mix containing salt, garlic powder, and red pepper and served heavily sauced. Meat-market pork is seasoned with nothing but salt, pepper, and smoke.

Because of its simplicity, meat-market barbecue is incredibly versatile. Smoky pork loin seasoned with only salt and pepper tastes good with barbecue sauce, potato salad, and coleslaw. But as I researched this cookbook, I wondered how it might taste if eaten the way the German Texans used to enjoy it—on a pile of sauerkraut. Fantastic is the answer!

Here are some German- and Czech-style Texas barbecue recipes, and some eccentric side dishes like *Apfelkraut*, red cabbage, and barbecued cabbage. You won't see these in a Texas barbecue joint, but they'll give you an idea of how German smoked meats and sausages were probably eaten in the old days.

J. R. MAC

CASH GR

MADE BY —
POCHYLA
AND
CHOVANEC.

GRANGER
TEXAS.

REPAIRED BY—
POCHYLA
AND
CHOVANEC.
GRANGER
TEXAS.

MADE BY —
POCHYLA
AND
CHOVANEC.

GRANGER
TEXAS.

Butchers and clerks in front of
J. R. Machu, a Czech grocery store
in Granger, 1903.

Barbecued Turkey

AT THANKSGIVING TIME, LOTS OF TEXANS TAKE THEIR TURKEYS TO THEIR favorite barbecue joints and have them smoked. Czech-Texan barbecuer Vencil Mares used to do a booming business smoking turkeys at his place in Taylor. He's retired from the turkey-smoking business now, but this is his recipe.

"Buy a fresh turkey," Vencil advises. "Season it up and add a bit of garlic and put it on the smoker. I do mine for four to five hours, but it all depends on your heat. At low heat, it takes a much longer time. Smoking a turkey is just like smoking a big pork roast." You'll do best with the smallest turkey you can find.

1 small turkey (12 to 13 pounds)
¼ cup dry rub of your choice
3 garlic cloves, minced

½ onion
3 cups Wish-Bone Italian dressing

Remove the giblets from the turkey and reserve for another use. Season the turkey inside and out with the dry rub and rub in well. Spread the garlic around inside the cavity.

Set up your smoker for indirect heat with a water pan, and put the onion in the water pan. Use wood chips, chunks, or logs, and keep up a good level of smoke. Maintain a temperature between 275° and 300°F.

Place the turkey, breast-side down, in the smoker as far away from the fire as possible. Cook the turkey for 2 hours, then turn it breast-side up, with the drumsticks pointing toward the fire, and baste it with some of the Italian dressing. After 2 hours more, rotate the turkey so that the drumsticks point away from the fire and baste it with more Italian dressing, leaving some in the cavity. Continue cooking and basting and regularly checking for doneness until a thermometer inserted into the thickest part of the thigh away from the bone registers 160°F. The timing will depend on the size of the bird.

Let the turkey rest for 15 minutes before carving.

SERVES 8 TO 10

Variations:

Aluminum Foil Wrap. Barbecued turkey gets nearly black before it cooks through. Just cover the bird in aluminum foil when it is brown enough to keep the color from getting too dark.

Spatchcocked Turkey. Split the turkey along either side of the backbone and remove the backbone. "Butterfly" the remaining turkey by spreading it apart and flattening the breast as much as possible. Proceed as directed, decreasing the cooking time.

Lockhart Pork Loin

KREUZ MARKET AND SMITTY'S IN LOCKHART both serve smoked pork loin cooked over a hot oak fire and seasoned with just salt and pepper. It's one of the best things to barbecue at home because it's so simple.

By leaving the bone in, you get a juicier roast. If you're going to use a Weber or a smaller barbecue smoker, go ahead and get a boneless pork loin roast. It will cut the cooking time down to about 2½ hours and save you some refueling. Slice the roast and accompany with barbecue sauce and fixin's, Southern style, or fan the slices over a platter of Apfelkraut (page 133) or Red Cabbage (page 132) and serve with German Potato Salad (page 127).

1 bone-in center-cut pork loin roast (about 4 pounds; ask the butcher to cut the bone at ½-inch intervals for easy slicing)

Salt and freshly ground black pepper

Set up your smoker for indirect heat with a water pan. Use wood chips, chunks, or logs, and keep up a good level of smoke. Maintain a temperature between 275° and 325°F.

Season the pork roast all over with salt and pepper and place it in the smoker. Allow it to smoke for several hours, rotating it every 30 minutes to expose all sides to the heat. After 2 hours, begin checking the temperature when you turn the roast. Cook until the pork reaches an internal temperature of 145°F for medium. Allow the roast to rest for 15 minutes; it should register 160°F. Slice between the bones to serve.

SERVES 6

The Family Feud in Lockhart

The meat market at 208 South Commerce in Lockhart was known as Kreuz Market when it opened in 1900. Edgar Schmidt, a.k.a. Smitty, started working at the meat market in 1935. In 1948, he bought the business and kept the Kreuz name. In 1984, sons Rick and Don Schmidt bought the business from their dad and expanded the barbecue operation.

Rick and Don's sister, Nina Sells, owns the building that houses the business. In 1999, Nina and Rick were unable to come to terms on a new lease, and Rick moved the business, Kreuz Market, to a new, much larger location down the street. Meanwhile, Nina kept the old meat market in business under the name Smitty's.

This family feud generated widespread publicity, including a front-page story in the *Austin American-Statesman* and a segment on a television news magazine. John Fullilove, Nina Sells's son, put the whole family feud story in a different perspective. "Kreuz Market outgrew this location," he said. "And now they have a great big, new place."

In 2011, Rick Schmidt sold Kreuz Market to his son, Keith Schmidt.

Bryan Bracewell
SOUTHSIDE MARKET

Bryan Bracewell, a third-generation barbecue man and graduate of Texas A&M, is the owner and pitmaster at the legendary Southside Market in Elgin.

Bryan Bracewell's Venison Sausage

EARLY HISTORIES OF THE HILL COUNTRY NOTE that the German immigrants had a tough time in their first few years due to crop failures and the fact that they weren't very good with firearms. Luckily, they were great butchers, so they ended up specializing in processing wild game for others.

5 pounds boneless fatty pork shoulder (also known as Boston butt), cut into strips

5 pounds boneless venison shoulder, cut into pieces

½ cup kosher salt

½ cup ground black pepper

1 pint pickled jalapeño slices with the juice

Vegetable oil for frying

Medium hog casings (available at butcher shops)

Grind the pork and venison together through the ¼-inch plate of a meat grinder (the chili plate). A little at a time, add the salt, pepper, and pickled jalapeño slices and juice as you go, so that they become well incorporated into the meat. In a large bowl, knead the mixture with your hands until everything is well blended.

In a small skillet, heat a little vegetable oil. Form a meatball-size piece of the mixture into a small patty and fry it. Taste for seasoning and adjust as needed.

Soak the hog casings in lukewarm water. Using a sausage stuffer or a pastry bag, stuff the meat mixture into the hog casings and tie into 4- to 6-inch links. (It will keep refrigerated for 3 to 4 days, or frozen for up to 2 months.)

When you're ready to cook the sausages, poach them in warm (140°F) water for 10 minutes, or until the meat mixture sets. Set up your smoker with wood chips or chunks at 275°F. Sear the links on a grate over hot coals for 3 minutes on each side, or until nicely browned. Move them to indirect heat over a drip pan and smoke for 30 minutes, or until cooked through. Serve hot.

MAKES 10 POUNDS

German Potato Salad

SERVE THIS SWEET-AND-SOUR POTATO SALAD WARM WITH A GARNISH OF crumbled bacon.

2½ pounds baby red potatoes
15 thin slices bacon
1 cup diced red onion
½ cup packed brown sugar

2 tablespoons cider vinegar
¾ cup olive oil
Kosher salt and freshly ground black pepper

Place the potatoes in a saucepan, add water to cover by 1½ inches, and bring to a boil over high heat. Turn the heat to low and simmer for 20 minutes, or until the potatoes are tender when tested with a knife.

While the potatoes are cooking, fry the bacon in a skillet over medium heat for 10 to 12 minutes, or until browned and crisp. Transfer to paper towels to drain. Pour off all but 2 tablespoons of the bacon fat from the skillet and return the pan to medium heat. Add the onion and sauté for about 10 minutes, or until softened. Transfer to a small bowl and set aside. Crumble the bacon.

Just before the potatoes are ready, in a large salad bowl, whisk together the brown sugar and vinegar until the sugar dissolves, then slowly add the olive oil while continuing to whisk to form a dressing. Season with salt and pepper. Add the onion and 1 cup of the bacon.

Drain the potatoes thoroughly, add them to the dressing, and toss to coat evenly. Let the salad sit at room temperature for 30 minutes, then garnish with the remaining bacon and serve warm.

SERVES 6

Variation:
German Sweet Potato Salad. Substitute peeled sweet potato cut into 1-inch dice for the baby red potatoes and proceed as directed.

Mayonnaise Myths

Forget the urban myth about the mess sergeant who poisoned his entire platoon that had been on maneuvers all day by serving them potato salad. Commercial mayonnaise uses pasteurized eggs and contains acids (vinegar, lemon, and salt) that actually kill bacteria that grow in food. Homemade mayonnaise is another scenario, but it would be heresy to use it in potato salad.

The cook is a more likely culprit in mass outbreaks of food poisoning. Adding cold mayonnaise to hot potatoes sets up a prime breeding ground for bacteria, which flourish at 40° to 145°F. Instead, refrigerate potato salad as soon as it's prepared to cool it down quickly. For the best flavor, remove it from the refrigerator and allow it to come to room temperature before serving.

—Beverly Bundy, Fort Worth food writer

Mustard Potato Salad

YOUR CHOICE OF MUSTARD MAKES A BIG difference in this recipe. In West Texas, folks like bright-yellow potato salad, so cooks use a yellow mustard like French's. German coarse-grain mustard gives the potato salad a darker color and a heartier flavor. French Dijon mustard makes it pretty hot.

8 russet potatoes
8 hard-boiled eggs, peeled and chopped
1 cup chopped onion
1 cup chopped celery
3 tablespoons chopped fresh parsley

2 teaspoons celery seeds
2 tablespoons prepared mustard
2½ cups mayonnaise
Salt and ground black pepper

Place the potatoes in a large pot, add water to cover generously, and bring to a boil over high heat. Turn the heat to low and simmer for 20 to 30 minutes, or until the potatoes are tender when tested with a knife.

Drain the potatoes, let cool until still slightly hot, then peel and cut into rough chunks. Transfer to a large bowl; add the eggs, onion, celery, parsley, celery seeds, mustard, and mayonnaise; and stir gently to mix well. Season with salt and pepper.

Serve chilled or at room temperature.

SERVES 12

Coleslaw

THE AMERICAN WORD *COLESLAW* COMES FROM THE DUTCH WORDS *KOOL*, meaning "cabbage," and *sla*, meaning "salad." Here's a simple recipe for old-fashioned Texas coleslaw. If you want to jazz it up, shredded carrots are a traditional addition. Shredded apples are a German addition that is particularly good with pork.

6 cups shredded cabbage	2 teaspoons salt
¼ cup distilled white vinegar	1 tablespoon sugar
½ cup mayonnaise	1 teaspoon ground black pepper

In a bowl, combine all of the ingredients, mixing well. Cover and refrigerate for a couple of hours before serving to allow the flavors to mellow.

SERVES 8

Variations:
Summer Slaw. For a lighter, pickled flavor that's perfect for summer picnics, omit the mayonnaise and add 1 teaspoon celery seeds.
Sauerkraut Slaw. Substitute fresh sauerkraut (available in pillow packs in the deli case) for the cabbage and omit the mayonnaise.

Uncle Kermit's Barbecued Cabbage

HERE'S AN OLD GERMAN RECIPE HANDED DOWN BY KERMIT SAKEWITZ, the uncle of a barbecue cook-off competitor I met in Taylor. If you have room on the smoker while you're barbecuing something else, give this a try.

1 head green cabbage
½ cup butter, plus more for serving
1 tablespoon salt

1 teaspoon ground black pepper
1 teaspoon garlic powder
1 teaspoon onion powder

Using a sharp knife, core the cabbage, removing a good-size chunk of the tough white bottom, then pull off any wilted or discolored leaves. Put the butter on a dinner plate and sprinkle the salt, pepper, garlic powder, and onion powder over it. Roll the butter around until all the spices stick to it. (You may need to let it soften a little.) Shove the spiced butter into the hole where the cabbage core was removed.

Wrap the cabbage in aluminum foil and turn the head core-end up. Use some excess foil to form a base that will keep the cabbage standing upright. Place on a smoker when smoking other items and cook for 4 to 6 hours, or until the cabbage is soft.

Unwrap the cabbage and discard any blackened leaves before serving. Cut into quarters and serve with additional butter.

SERVES 4

A young German butcher in
Texas in the early 1900s.

Red Cabbage

IMMERSING THE CABBAGE IN A BRINE AND WORKING IT WITH YOUR HANDS before cooking will give it a beautiful deep color. The sweet-and-sour flavor of German red cabbage is an interesting alternative to barbecue sauce with a simple smoked pork loin, smoked pork chops, or barbecued sausage.

1 large head red cabbage

1 tablespoon salt

2 tablespoons butter

1 large onion, chopped

2 large Granny Smith apples, peeled, cored, and chopped

2 tablespoons all-purpose flour

1 tablespoon sugar, or to taste

1 cup red wine

¼ cup red wine vinegar, or to taste

1 cup beef stock

2 bay leaves

¼ cup strawberry jam

Quarter the cabbage through the stem end, cut away the core section from each quarter, and pull off any wilted or discolored leaves. Thinly slice each cabbage quarter crosswise. Fill a large bowl or nonreactive pot with warm water, add the salt, and stir to dissolve. Put the cabbage in the salted water and work it with your hands until the water turns an intense purple. Allow the cabbage to marinate in the colored water at room temperature for several hours, or up to overnight.

If you have used a bowl for marinating the cabbage, transfer the cabbage and its soaking water to a nonreactive pot. Place the pot over medium-high heat, bring to a boil, and boil for about 5 minutes, or until the cabbage is tender-crisp. Drain and discard the water.

In a Dutch oven, melt the butter over medium-high heat. Add the onion and sauté for 5 to 7 minutes, or until soft. Add the apples and continue cooking, stirring often, for about 5 minutes, or until the apples soften. Add the cooked cabbage, sprinkle the flour and sugar over it, and toss the cabbage to coat evenly. Add the wine, vinegar, stock, and bay leaves and simmer for 15 minutes, until the cabbage is soft and the mixture has thickened.

Add the jam and taste for seasoning. If you like an intense sweet-and-sour taste, you will need to add more vinegar and sugar. Transfer to a serving bowl and serve immediately.

SERVES 8

Apfelkraut

"MY MAMA'S FAMILY WAS BOHEMIAN; MY GRANDMOTHER USED TO SERVE smoked sausage and sauerkraut all the time," Norma Moore of Cuero told me one day while she was buying sausage at Smolik's. But the Bohemians didn't eat sauerkraut straight out of the barrel (or can) the way Americans do. They cooked it with other ingredients to give it flavor, with apples, white wine, and bacon being a few of the most common additions.

Here's an old-world apple kraut that's great served with smoked pork sausage or pork loin. Avoid serving this with heavily smoked meats, as the smoky flavor will overwhelm the kraut.

15 juniper berries

3 bay leaves

10 black peppercorns

3 tablespoons vegetable oil

4 cups chopped onion

2 garlic cloves, minced

6 cups fresh sauerkraut (available in pillow packs in the deli case)

3 McIntosh or other sweet cooking apples, peeled, cored, and cut into ½-inch dice

2 cups apple juice

¼ cup cider vinegar

3 tablespoons sugar

Smoked sausage, smoked ribs, and/or smoked pork for serving

Put the juniper berries, bay leaves, and peppercorns on a square of cheesecloth, bring the corners together, and tie securely with kitchen string to make a bouquet garni. In a Dutch oven, heat the vegetable oil over high heat. Add the onion and sauté for 5 minutes, or until it begins to wilt. Add the garlic, mix well, and then add the bouquet garni, sauerkraut, and apples and stir well to combine. Add the apple juice, vinegar, and sugar and bring the mixture to a boil, stirring occasionally. Turn the heat to low and simmer for 1 hour, or until the sauerkraut is very tender.

Uncover and remove and discard the bouquet garni. Increase the heat to high, bring to a boil, and boil until the liquid has reduced and the mixture holds together. Transfer to a large platter, top with the meat, and serve.

SERVES 6

CELEBRATING JUNETEENTH

The Legacy of East Texas

Carving barbecue to sell at a
booth at the Gonzales County Fair,
1939. *Photo by Russell Lee*

frican slaves introduced many cooking traditions to Texas, including the Southern version of barbecue. As cotton growers moved into the fertile river bottoms and blacklands of East Texas, by 1860, slaves began to represent a significant percentage of the state's population.

On June 19, 1865, Union soldiers, led by Major General Gordon Granger, landed at Galveston and announced that the slaves were free. African-Americans in Texas have celebrated the anniversary of their freedom on that day ever since.

In a 1938 interview with a Works Progress Administration (WPA) writer, former slave Anderson Jones remembered the original freedom celebrations, in which "hogs and cattle" were barbecued. "I kin remember w'en I was jes a boy about nine years old w'en freedom cum's . . . w'en we commenced to have de nineteenth celebrations . . . an' everybody seem's like, w'ite an' black cum an' git some barbecue."

In the late 1800s, African-Americans in Texas celebrated Juneteenth, as the June 19 anniversary of emancipation became known, with large outdoor gatherings. These events sometimes included rodeos, prayer meetings, baseball games, and guest speakers, but they always included barbecue picnics.

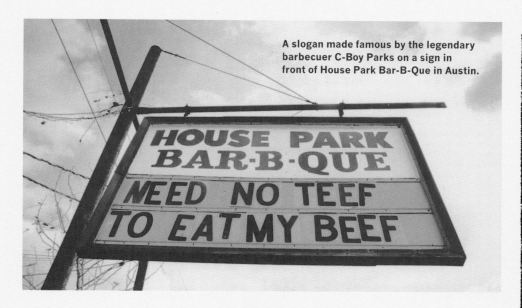

A slogan made famous by the legendary barbecuer C-Boy Parks on a sign in front of House Park Bar-B-Que in Austin.

Barbecuing was considered a tradition that was handed down directly from the celebrations of the freed slaves.

Pork, mutton, goat, and wild game were the original barbecue meats in cotton country. Today, barbecued mutton is still seen in East Texas. But here, as in the rest of the South, pork is the reigning favorite. As with Southern barbecue, the meats are preferred falling-off-the-bone tender and more heavily sauced.

Although East Texas barbecue draws heavily on Southern barbecue tradition, it has its own distinct style. East Texas is the only place where black Southern barbecue includes beef. Brisket in East Texas is often smothered in sauce after it is smoked and then simmered until it falls apart. The barbecued beef sausage of East Texas, known as beef links, is made with finely ground beef, beef fat, and paprika. East Texas barbecue joints also tend to be proud of their side dishes, including old Southern classics like turnip greens, okra, fried green tomatoes, and others not seen in barbecue restaurants elsewhere in Texas.

Juneteenth celebrations almost died out in the early 1900s, when the Fourth of July rose in importance as a civic celebration. But when Ralph Abernathy and other civil rights leaders called for an official holiday celebrating African-American emancipation, Juneteenth made a revival. Thanks to the efforts of African-Americans in the Texas legislature, on January 1, 1980, Juneteenth became a state holiday in Texas. In the last thirty years, several other states have adopted Juneteenth as a state holiday, as well. As the celebration of Juneteenth spreads across the country, African-Texan barbecue traditions will surely follow.

Sam's Mutton

SAM'S IS ONE OF THE LAST BARBECUE JOINTS IN TEXAS THAT STILL SERVES mutton seven days a week. Wanda, Joseph, and Willie Mays, the second generation of the Mays family to operate the place, inherited the tradition of barbecued mutton from founder Sam Mays. They told me that they smoke mutton for five to six hours, but they wouldn't tell me the ingredients of their secret seasoning mix.

1 square-cut lamb shoulder roast (7 to 8 pounds)

2 tablespoons Louis Charles Henley's All-Purpose Rub (facing page)

Sprinkle the meat all over with the rub and press it into the meat.

Set up your smoker for indirect heat with a water pan. Use wood chips, chunks, or logs, and keep up a good level of smoke. Maintain a temperature between 225° and 275°F.

Place the lamb in the smoker and cook for 6 to 7 hours, turning it often so it cooks evenly. The meat is done when the internal temperature reaches 190°F and it pulls easily away from the bone. Serve immediately.

SERVES 4

Louis Charles Henley's All-Purpose Rub

"I USE THE SAME RUB FOR PORK, BEEF, AND mutton," says pitmaster Louis Charles Henley. "A lot of people like to put sugar in a seasoning rub for pork. Me, I've gotten away from that. Sugar sticks to the grill, and it can give the meat a burnt taste. And in the heat of the summer, it speeds up the spoiling process, too. I don't use MSG anymore, either. It makes the meat tender, but too many people are allergic to it." Here's Louis's suggestion for a simple rub that you can use on everything.

¼ cup Lawry's Seasoning
   Salt
1 tablespoon ground black
   pepper
2 teaspoons garlic powder
1 teaspoon chili powder

Combine all of the ingredients in a shaker bottle, cap tightly, and shake the bottle to mix well. Store at room temperature for up to 1 month.

MAKES 6 TABLESPOONS

Pulled Pork

PULLED PORK IS THE EXTREMELY TENDER SHREDDED MEAT FROM A long-cooked pork cut. Originally, pulled pork included mixed meats from an entire hog. But in East Texas, pork shoulder has largely replaced the whole animal. In supermarket meat cases, whole pork shoulders are divided into two cuts, the meaty Boston butt and the pork picnic, which is covered with skin and includes the end of the shoulder bone. The Boston butt is the more popular of the two because of its better yield. But for juicier pulled pork, try a pork picnic with the skin left on. Freeze seasoned pulled pork in airtight (or, better yet, vacuum-packed) plastic packages divided into 1-pound or 2-pound portions.

1 bone-in Boston butt or pork picnic (4 to 5 pounds)

6 tablespoons Stubb's Hot Pork Rub (facing page)

2 onions, halved

3 cups Klassic Mop (page 74)

Kosher salt and ground black pepper

Gatlin's Vinegar Pepper Sauce for Pork for seasoning (page 144)

Sprinkle the meat all over with the rub, pressing the rub into the meat. Wrap in plastic wrap and refrigerate overnight. The next day, unwrap the meat and bring it to room temperature before putting it in the smoker.

Set up your smoker for indirect heat with a water pan, and put the onions in the water pan. Use wood chips, chunks, or logs and keep up a good level of smoke. Maintain a temperature between 210° and 250°F.

Place the pork in the smoker. After the first 2 hours, mop the pork every 30 minutes with the mop sauce, turning the meat at the same time so it will cook evenly. The pork is ready when an instant-read thermometer inserted into the center away from the bone registers 200°F. This will take about 12 hours total.

Transfer the roast to a cutting board and let rest until it is cool enough to handle. Then, pull the pork from the bone, removing and discarding any big chunks of gristle as you go. Shred the meat by hand and season with salt, pepper, and vinegar pepper sauce. Use immediately, or transfer to an airtight container and store in the refrigerator for up to 1 week.

MAKES ABOUT 3 POUNDS

Variation:
Gatlin's Pulled Pork Sandwich. Pile 5 to 6 ounces pork on the bottom of a toasted hamburger bun, add a few pickle and onion slices, and top with coleslaw, if desired. Serve with extra vinegar pepper sauce on the side.

Stubb's Hot Pork Rub

STUBBS—C. B. STUBBLEFIELD—HAS PASSED AWAY, BUT STUBB'S BARBECUE IN Austin tries to keep his spirit alive. This is the restaurant's recipe for hot pork rub.

1 cup salt
¼ cup chili powder
¼ cup paprika
⅓ cup garlic powder

⅓ cup cayenne pepper
½ cup ground dried rosemary
½ cup ground black pepper

Combine all of the ingredients in a shaker bottle, cap tightly, and shake the bottle to mix well. Store at room temperature for up to 1 month.

MAKES ABOUT 3 CUPS

Greg Gatlin

Pitmaster Greg Gatlin runs Gatlin's BBQ on 3510 Ella Boulevard in Houston, just north of downtown. He is also a partner in Jackson Street Barbecue next to Minute Maid Park, home of the Houston Astros. The Gatlin family has ties to western Louisiana, so they serve Texas barbecue with a Creole accent.

Gatlin's Vinegar Pepper Sauce for Pork

GREG GATLIN'S FAMILY IS FROM LOUISIANA, SO he is no stranger to Southern-style pork barbecue. At his family's barbecue joint in Houston, you'll also find Texas brisket, several kinds of sausage, and two kinds of pork ribs, along with pulled pork and Louisiana sides like dirty rice. "We want to keep everybody happy," he says. This is an adaptation of Gatlin's vinegar sauce. Try it on a pulled pork sandwich.

1 cup sherry vinegar

2 cups rice vinegar

1 shot dark rum

2 tablespoons kosher salt

1 tablespoon cane syrup or molasses

1 tablespoon coarsely ground black pepper

3 serrano chiles, halved lengthwise

2 carrot spears

In a saucepan, combine the sherry vinegar, rice vinegar, rum, salt, cane syrup, and black pepper; place over medium heat; and heat, stirring, until the salt and syrup are dissolved. Remove from the heat and let cool.

Transfer the cooled liquid to a 1-quart liquor bottle with a cap, then drop the chiles and carrots through the mouth of the bottle and cap tightly. Store in the refrigerator for up to 3 months—it gets better with age.

MAKES ABOUT 3½ CUPS

Monte Barber's
Country-Style Ribs

MONTE BARBER WAS THE PITMASTER AT STUBB'S BAR-B-Q ON RED RIVER Street in Austin when I stopped by. Barber gave me this recipe for country-style ribs; he says that a pork roast won't fit on his little smoker at home, but these ribs fit perfectly. Country-style ribs are actually pork shoulder (Boston butt) roasts cut into strips. They are very meaty, and they take a long time to cook. Don't be in a rush. To locate Stubb's Bar-B-Q Sauce, see Online and Mail-Order Sources on page 288.

2 cups orange juice

1 cup Stubb's Bar-B-Q Sauce or the
   barbecue sauce of your choice

3 pounds country-style pork ribs

3 tablespoons Stubb's Hot Pork Rub
   (page 143)

Combine the orange juice and barbecue sauce in a resealable plastic freezer bag, add the meat, seal closed, and refrigerate overnight. The next day, remove the meat from the marinade and let it dry at room temperature. Sprinkle the ribs with the rub and press it into the meat.

Set up your smoker for indirect heat with a water pan. Use wood chips, chunks, or logs, and keep up a good level of smoke. Maintain a temperature between 225° and 275°F.

Place the ribs in the smoker and cook them, turning them every 30 minutes so they cook evenly. They should be ready in 4 to 5 hours. The meat is done when it pulls easily away from the bone, but don't worry about overcooking it. It will just keep getting better. An internal temperature of around 170°F is perfect. Serve hot.

SERVES 4 TO 6

Joe Burney

Houston pitmaster Joe Burney as remembered by his daughter, Karen Mayberry: "My father was born March 5, 1903, in Baldwin, Louisiana. He moved to Houston and got a job 'in service,' which meant working as a driver, porter, manservant in those days. He worked for a man named Bob Smith. The Third Ward was a booming African-American business district in the late 1940s. My mom and dad saved their money and bought the Avalon BBQ in the 2700 block of Dowling, which they owned with two other black barbecue men, Oscar Lott and Bill Williams. The small BBQ joint was famous for ribs and links, and my dad worked hard to build up a good reputation. He learned to cook juicy links from Matt Garner, one of the old-timers around here.

"My dad used to drive around and give away barbecue to old folks who couldn't get out of the house. When the Avalon burned down, he used

Joe Burney's Juicy Links

ACCORDING TO HOUSTON BARBECUE VETERAN Harry Green, beef links aren't as good as they used to be because people don't like all the orange grease that flows out when you cut into them, so sausage makers are adding too little fat. The original recipe at Burney's BBQ called for a combination of beef scraps and suet ground together in a ratio of 70 percent meat to 30 percent suet.

¼ cup salt
¼ cup paprika
2 tablespoons ground black pepper
1 tablespoon garlic powder
3½ pounds beef shoulder clod or beef scraps, cut into pieces

1½ pounds suet (beef fat), cut into pieces
Medium hog casings (available at butcher shops)

In a small bowl, stir together the salt, paprika, pepper, and garlic powder. Grind the beef and suet together through the fine plate of a meat grinder, adding the spice mix a little at a time as you go. Transfer the ground meat to a large stand mixer fitted with the paddle attachment and beat on medium speed until extremely well combined. Cover and refrigerate the mixture for at least an hour.

Soak the hog casings in lukewarm water. Using a sausage stuffer or a pastry bag, stuff the meat mixture into the hog casings and tie into 4- to 6-inch links. The sausage will keep refrigerated for 3 to 4 days, or frozen for up to 2 months.

When you're ready to cook the sausages, set up your smoker for indirect heat. Smoke the beef links at 250°F for 35 to 45 minutes, turning them to cook them evenly. Serve hot.

MAKES ABOUT 5 POUNDS

House Park Pork Loin Sandwiches

AUSTIN'S HOUSE PARK IS A TINY BARBECUE JOINT named after the high school football stadium next door. Eating one of its pork loin sandwiches at a picnic table out front near 12th Street is an Austin tradition. For a new twist, try the pork loin sandwiched between slices of fried green tomato (see page 148) in place of the bun.

1 cup barbecue sauce of
    your choice
1 pound Lockhart Pork Loin
    (page 125), warm or
    at room temperature

4 hamburger buns, split
Salt and ground black pepper
½ sweet onion, thinly sliced
8 pickle slices

Heat the barbecue sauce in a small saucepan over low heat until hot.

Cut the loin against the grain into thin slices. Dip the cut side of the bottom half of each hamburger bun in the barbecue sauce and place, cut-side up, on individual plates. Layer the loin slices onto the bun bottoms, dividing evenly and sprinkling with salt and pepper as you pile. Top with the onion and pickle slices, then dip the cut sides of the bun tops in the barbecue sauce and place atop the sandwiches. Serve immediately.

SERVES 4

the insurance money to build Burney's BBQ on Holman. It became an iconic African-American BBQ spot in late 1940s Houston. Unkie Lott started his own place called Lott's Barbecue on Holman. Bill Williams opened another place on Scott. My mother and father cooked in the evening and worked their regular jobs during the day. The day crew sold the barbecue.

"My father did very well. He bought some show horses and he was very proud of them. There was a group of black businessmen that supported one another. They formed a club called the El Dorado Social Club. It became the center of the social scene in the Third Ward. It's still around today.

"My father died on October 12, 1958. I was six when it happened. My mom ran the barbecue joint for a year, then sold Burney's to Harry Green—my dad taught Harry Green to cook at Burney's. I got a job at Lott's Barbecue when I was old enough to work. That's where I met my husband, Waymon Mayberry; he worked there too. I married a barbecue man, of course."

Fried Green Tomatoes

SOME FOLKS LIKE TO MAKE THEIR PORK LOIN SANDWICHES WITH FRIED green tomatoes, layering the pork and barbecue sauce between two tomato slices. Pick it up if you want, or eat it with a fork and knife.

Peanut oil for deep frying
1 cup fine-grind cornmeal
Salt and ground white pepper

2 eggs
2 tablespoons water
4 green tomatoes, thickly sliced

Into a heavy-bottomed pot, pour the peanut oil to a depth of 1 inch and heat to 350°F. Set a wire rack on a baking sheet and place next to the stove.

Spread the cornmeal on a plate and season with salt and white pepper. Crack the eggs into a shallow dish, such as a pie plate, add the water, and beat with a fork just until blended.

One at a time, drop the tomato slices into the egg mixture and then dredge them in the cornmeal to coat, tapping off the excess.

Working in batches, add the tomato slices to the hot oil and fry, turning them once, for 2 to 3 minutes, or until golden brown on both sides. Using tongs, transfer them to the wire rack and let cool slightly. Serve immediately.

MAKES ABOUT 12 TOMATO SLICES

Mashed Potato Salad

POTATO SALAD IS SOFT AND FLUFFY IN EAST TEXAS. AT THE NEW ZION Missionary Baptist Church Barbecue in Huntsville, it is served with an ice-cream scoop. It tastes best when it's still warm.

1½ pounds russet potatoes, peeled and cut into 1-inch chunks
½ cup mayonnaise
2 green onions, sliced

1 tablespoon pickle relish
4 teaspoons pickle juice
4 teaspoons hot-pepper sauce
Salt

Place the potatoes in a large saucepan, add water to cover generously, and bring to a boil over high heat. Turn the heat to medium-low, cover, and simmer for 15 minutes, or until the potatoes are tender.

Drain the potatoes well, transfer to a large bowl, and mash coarsely. Stir in the mayonnaise, green onions, pickle relish, pickle juice, and pepper sauce, mixing well, then season with salt. Serve slightly warm or refrigerate, then allow to come to room temperature before serving.

SERVES 4

Passing the time in front of New Zion Missionary Baptist Church Barbecue in Huntsville.

Lloyd Bentsen Highway Rice Salad

BARBECUE JOINTS IN THE RICE-GROWING REGION ALONG HIGHWAY 59 (Lloyd Bentsen Highway), between Houston and Victoria, all serve some kind of rice salad along with the usual potato and macaroni salads. Here's a modern version.

3 cups freshly cooked Texmati rice

½ cup vinaigrette or Italian dressing

½ cup chopped tomato

½ cup chopped celery

½ cup chopped green bell pepper

¼ cup diced carrot

¼ cup chopped red onion

1 cup peeled, seeded, and chopped cucumber

½ cup chopped black olives

1 tablespoon hot-pepper sauce

1 teaspoon prepared mustard

½ cup plain yogurt

½ cup chopped toasted pecans

3 tablespoons chopped fresh cilantro

In a large bowl, toss the rice with the vinaigrette and refrigerate just until the rice is cool.

Remove the rice from the refrigerator; add the tomato, celery, bell pepper, carrot, onion, cucumber, olives, pepper sauce, mustard, and yogurt; and stir and toss to mix well. Garnish with the pecans and cilantro and serve at room temperature.

SERVES 8

Leon's Stepped-Up Rice

IF YOU WANT SOMETHING DIFFERENT FROM THE USUAL BEANS OR POTATO salad, try this tasty rice dish, which Leon O'Neal offers at his In & Out B-B-Q House on Galveston Island.

3 jalapeño chiles, seeded and
   coarsely chopped
1 onion, coarsely chopped
3 celery stalks, chopped

1 green bell pepper, seeded and chopped
2 tablespoons peanut oil
4 cups freshly cooked Texmati rice
Salt and ground black pepper

Combine the jalapeños, onion, celery, and bell pepper in a food processor and pulse just until reduced to a finely chopped paste.

In a large skillet, heat the peanut oil over medium heat. Add the vegetable paste and cook, stirring often, for 5 to 7 minutes, or until soft. Add the rice and stir and toss until evenly mixed with the vegetable paste. Season with salt and pepper. Serve immediately.

SERVES 4 TO 6

Leon O'Neal's Turnip Greens

AT LEON'S "WORLD'S FINEST" IN & OUT B-B-Q HOUSE ON GALVESTON ISLAND, they serve tender ribs and tangy sauce with sensational Southern-style vegetables. "It's all in the seasoning," says Leon. Here's his recipe for turnip greens.

1 large bunch turnip greens
1 small turnip, peeled and diced
Pinch of sugar
6 slices bacon, diced

1 onion, diced
1 tablespoon lemon pepper
Salt
Louisiana hot sauce for serving

Turnip greens often conceal lots of dirt, so wash well in several changes of water until no more grit is visible. Chop the greens coarsely. Bring a large pot of water to a boil; add the greens, turnip, and sugar; and cook for 12 to 15 minutes, or until tender. Drain well.

In a large skillet, sauté the bacon over medium heat until it renders its fat. Add the onion and cook for about 7 minutes, or until the onion is soft. Add the drained vegetables and toss with the bacon and onion, mixing well and heating through. Add the lemon pepper and season with salt.

Transfer to a serving dish and serve immediately. Pass the hot sauce at the table.

SERVES 4

Variation:
Green Beans. Substitute 1 pound green beans, trimmed and snapped in half, for the turnip greens and omit the sugar. Proceed as directed.

Huntsville Butter Beans

YOU'LL FIND PINTO BEANS SERVED WITH BARBECUE ALL OVER THE STATE, but the New Zion Missionary Baptist Church Barbecue is the only place I've had Southern-style lima beans, a.k.a. butter beans.

1 pound dried lima beans

1 onion, diced

1 ham hock, or 6 slices bacon, diced

Salt and ground black pepper

    Pick over the beans and rinse well. Place in a bowl, add water to cover generously, and let soak overnight.

    Drain the beans, discard the water, and transfer the beans to a slow cooker. Add the onion, ham hock, and water to cover. Cook on the high setting for 1 hour, then turn the heat to low and cook for 4 to 5 hours, or until meltingly tender. Season with salt and pepper and serve hot.

SERVES 6

THE LAST
OF THE
OPEN PITS

Mutton ribs on an open pit at the Millheim Harmonie Verein, an old German dance hall near Sealy.

he open-pit barbecue tradition that was brought to Texas by Southern cotton-plantation owners and their slaves is still alive today. Just north of where the state's earliest cotton culture was established in Stephen F. Austin's colony, meat is still barbecued in open pits.

Ironically, it's not Southerners or African-Americans who preserved the old ways, but the immigrant groups that opposed slavery and secession in the Civil War era. German *Verein* societies, Czech Catholic churches, and Sons of Hermann Halls in the region of the old Austin Colony and the original state capital of Washington on the Brazos still hold annual community barbecues that look amazingly similar to the open-pit barbecue style of a century ago. If you want to see what old-fashioned Southern pit barbecue once looked like, visit one of these events early in the morning just before the meat comes off the fire.

In the ghost town of Millheim, there is an old German dance hall called the Millheim Harmonie Verein that dates to August 30, 1872. Members of the society gather at the hall every year on Father's Day to cook eight hundred pounds of barbecue for their annual fund-raiser. They claim their barbecue tradition goes back over a century, and after watching the men cook on the open pits, it's hard to argue otherwise.

Eating barbecue during a roundup at Sheriff Travis Hogue Pool's ranch in La Salle County, 1941.

Cowboy-style ribs are cooked directly over hot coals at a barbeque at the LBJ Ranch.

Until the 1960s, the pigs, calves, and sheep to be cooked were slaughtered on the spot, but not anymore. But the "barbecue gravy" is still cooked in cast-iron washtubs and stirred with boat paddles.

Old-fashioned mutton shoulder and mutton ribs, pork shoulder, and beef shoulder clod are the three meat choices. German-style red potatoes in butter and pinto beans are the sides, and plenty of white bread, raw onion slices, and pickles are always available. Beer is sold inside the splendidly preserved old wooden dance hall, along with desserts.

The Sons of Hermann Hall in Washington is another place to see barbecue cooked the old-fashioned way on a cinder-block open pit. Bubba Roese was the chairman of the barbecue committee the first year I stopped by. I asked him what he thought about Kreuz Market, Smitty's, and the German meat markets in Central Texas. "They aren't really cooking barbecue," Bubba said. "Barbecue isn't supposed to taste smoky."

Walter Jetton, who catered Lyndon Johnson's barbecues at the LBJ Ranch, also cooked on an open pit. The idea of enclosing the pit to capture the smoke was crazy, in Jetton's opinion.

Jetton came to the attention of the American public after catering a "barbecue state dinner" in honor of the president-elect of Mexico at the LBJ Ranch. In magazine articles and cookbooks, Jetton baffled Americans by insisting that if they wanted to make real Texas barbecue, they had to dig holes in their backyards. In one interview, he said,

"To barbecue, you need a pit . . . and it definitely shouldn't be one of those backyard creations with a chimney."

Jetton was also a proponent of slow cooking in open pits. In this style of barbecue, "low and slow" was indeed the only way to go. By using coals instead of flaming wood, you avoided flare-ups that would burn the meat. In the days when whole steers or forequarters were cut up for barbecuing, long, slow cooking was the only way to get the toughest cuts tender.

Eventually, Walter Jetton, like most Texas barbecuers, abandoned whole steer barbecue in favor of boxed beef cuts—especially brisket. In a letter to Larry Hunt, a lumberman in Minnesota who was looking for advice on barbecuing half steers, Jetton wrote, "First we would suggest you abandon the idea of a spit and instead of trying to barbecue the beef in quarters or halves, just buy eight- to ten-pound pieces of boneless brisket points." The fat layer attached to a brisket melts slowly as the meat cooks. Jetton called brisket a "self-basting cut."

Long after urban barbecue restaurants began to move their cooking into enclosed pits for sanitary reasons, West Texans continued to cook outdoors. Chuck-wagon cooks cooked meat over open fires and simmered beans in cast-iron Dutch ovens. That's why meat cooked over an open pit is often referred to as "cowboy barbecue."

Following are a few of Walter Jetton's recipes, in case you are planning a barbecue for 250 of your closest friends.

Walter Jetton's Barbecued Beef for 250

ALTHOUGH A BARBECUE FOR A COUPLE OF HUNDRED PEOPLE WAS NO BIG deal in Texas, the rest of the country was fascinated by the doings down at the LBJ Ranch. Magazines and newspapers featured Texas barbecue recipes, and the White House received letters asking for tips. Here's a recipe derived from Walter Jetton's advice.

35 top-quality beef briskets (about 10 pounds each) or 300 pounds beef, cut into 6- to 8-pound pieces
Salt and ground black pepper
10 pounds 32 Pounds of Dry Rub (page 166), or to taste

6 gallons Jetton's Beef Stock Mop (facing page)
Cold River Cattle Company BBQ Sauce for 250 (page 168), heated
Sandwich rolls, pickle slices, and onion slices for making sandwiches

Dig a pit 3 feet deep, 4 feet wide, and 40 feet long. Arrange a layer of wood (any type of hardwood can be used) across the bottom of the pit and start the fire. Keep the fire at the same height for about 5 hours and then let it die down to coals.

Place a length of iron pipe across the pit every 3 feet and then cover the pipe frame with heavy wire mesh. Tie the mesh securely in place so the meat won't get dumped into the fire. Make a 1-foot opening under the wire at regular intervals through which additional coals can be added. Start another fire to one side so that additional coals will be available.

Season the meat generously with salt and pepper and the rub and place the pieces on the wire mesh, being careful not to overlap them. You need to leave plenty of room for the smoke to come up. Cook the meat, basting it with the mop sauce every 30 minutes and turning it frequently so that it will cook evenly. Allow at least 18 hours' cooking time, and throw a little water on the coals once or twice during the cooking time to steam the meat with intense moist heat. Do not allow any blaze after the meat is put on—only coals! The meat is ready when it is fork tender.

Allow the meat to rest for 15 minutes before carving. Cut the meat into thin slices against the grain and serve with the barbecue sauce, rolls, pickles, and onions.

MAKES ENOUGH BARBECUED BEEF FOR SANDWICHES FOR 250

Jetton's Beef Stock Mop

JETTON STARTED HIS MOP SAUCE WITH A BEEF stock made from the bones left over from the butchering of the steer. He used a full-size cotton mop to baste hundreds of pounds of meat; for home cooks, however, he recommended miniature cotton mops used for dishwashing. Those little cotton mops aren't used much for dishes anymore, but you can still find them in stores selling barbecue and kitchen goods.

4 gallons beef stock
¾ cup salt
¾ cup MSG
¾ cup dry mustard
¾ cup paprika
½ cup garlic powder
½ cup chili powder
¼ cup ground bay leaf
½ cup hot-pepper sauce
2 quarts Worcestershire
    sauce
2 quarts vinegar
2 quarts vegetable oil

Combine all of the ingredients in a large vessel and stir well to dissolve the salt and MSG and mix the ingredients thoroughly. Let stand overnight before using to baste barbecued meats. Discard any leftover mop after using.

MAKES ABOUT 8 GALLONS

America's First State Barbecue

Menu for the barbecue given by President and Mrs. Lyndon B. Johnson honoring President-elect of Mexico Gustavo Díaz Ordaz and his wife, held on the banks of the Pedernales River at the LBJ Ranch at 1 P.M., Thursday, November 12, 1964.

Barbecued brisket
Barbecued pork ribs
Barbecued chicken
Hot links
Ranch-style beans
Sourdough biscuits
German potato salad
Texas coleslaw
Dill pickles
Sliced onions
Fried apple pie
Six-shooter coffee
and Iced tea

32 Pounds of Dry Rub

SALT COMES IN 25-POUND BAGS, SO MOST OF THE BARBECUE RUBS IN THE OLD days started with this quantity. Here's an old meat-market recipe for dry rub.

25 pounds salt

3 pounds coarsely ground black pepper

2 pounds sugar

1 pound chili powder

1 pound garlic powder

Combine all of the ingredients in a large vessel and mix well. Store in an airtight container at room temperature for up to 1 month. Rub on meats before barbecuing.

MAKES 32 POUNDS

Texas-Size Coleslaw

HERE'S A LARGE-QUANTITY RECIPE FOR OLD-FASHIONED COLESLAW. The salad gets better as it sits.

12 heads green cabbage, cored
and shredded

6 pounds carrots, peeled and shredded

2 cups sugar

¼ cup salt

2 tablespoons ground black pepper

1 tablespoon garlic powder

2 cups distilled white vinegar

8 cups mayonnaise

In a large food-grade plastic tub (or several smaller containers), combine all of the ingredients and mix well. Cover and allow to mellow in the refrigerator for a few hours before serving, mixing every 30 minutes. Store in the refrigerator for up to 4 days.

MAKES ABOUT 20 POUNDS

Walter Jetton serves up a plate to LBJ and guests at America's first barbecue state dinner.

A Cowboy Barbecue

"Nine months of the year . . . you didn't see hide nor hair of the headquarters. You saw the ramrod . . . you saw the foreman . . . but what you didn't see were any signs of civilization. I put in five years with about the same routine.

"We boys began hearing rumors that the railroad was going to have a big dance and barbecue when the end of the line reached O'Donnell, Texas [in 1912]. Well, that was all I wanted to know. A dance and a barbecue! At the end of the day, there was at least five thousand people there. Tons of meat was barbecued in advance, but not near enough."
—Frank March, WPA interview, 1938

Cold River Cattle Company BBQ Sauce for 250

RICHARD FLORES DOES THE COOKING FOR THE big parties at the Cold River Cattle Company Barbecue Team's Houston Livestock and Rodeo Barbecue Cook-Off booth. He also does a lot of catering jobs, so he tends to make a lot of barbecue sauce at one time. Here's his recipe for a large crowd.

Six #10 (114-ounce) cans ketchup
1½ gallons cider vinegar
1 gallon rice vinegar
Four 14-ounce cans chipotle chiles in adobo sauce

3 cups brown sugar
1 cup celery salt
½ cup ground black pepper
4 cups chopped garlic
4 cups chili powder
2 cups whole-grain mustard

In a large pot, combine all of the ingredients and place over a high propane fire. Bring to a boil, stirring until the sugar dissolves. Lower the heat to a simmer and cook, stirring frequently, for 15 minutes, or until slightly thickened.

Remove from the heat and process with a restaurant-size immersion blender. Use immediately, or let cool, transfer to airtight containers, and store in the refrigerator for up to 2 weeks.

MAKES ABOUT 6 GALLONS

Lorenzo Vences
COOPER'S OLD
TIME PIT BAR-B-Q

"Mesquite coals give the meat a lot of flavor without over-smoking it," says Lorenzo Vences, longtime pitmaster at Cooper's in Llano. "This is the best barbecue in Texas."

Lorenzo Vences's Sirloin

COOPER'S OLD TIME PIT BAR-B-Q PRESERVED the "cowboy barbecue" open-pit style. At Cooper's, mesquite wood is burned down to coals in a fireplace and then the coals are shoveled into enclosed pits. The meat is cooked by direct heat twenty-eight to thirty inches above the coals with the lid closed. When the steak is done to 140°F, it is moved to a holding pit where it continues to cook slowly until it is sold. Pitmaster Lorenzo Vences at Cooper's in Llano estimated the heat in his pit at 350° to 400°F.

1 USDA Choice beef sirloin steak (2 to 2½ pounds and 1¾ inches thick) or USDA Choice beef sirloin tip roast (2 to 2½ pounds; branded beef such as Black Angus or Certified Hereford preferred)

Salt and coarsely ground black pepper

Allow the meat to come to room temperature and season it all over with salt and pepper. Light mesquite chunks in a starter chimney. Pour the hot coals into your firebox. Light another batch of mesquite chunks a few minutes later. Maintain a temperature between 350° and 400°F.

Place the meat at least 18 inches directly above the coals and cook, turning once, until well browned and an instant-read thermometer inserted into the thickest part registers 120°F. Add more coals as needed to maintain the heat, and douse any flare-ups with a spray bottle.

When the steak is well charred, move it to a cooler part of the grate where it can cook indirectly until it reaches the desired temperature. For medium, remove it from the smoker when it is firm to the touch, between 135° and 140°F. The meat will continue to cook after it is removed; allow it to rest before carving. Remove the meat at 145°F for medium-well and 155°F for well-done.

SERVES 4 TO 6

Variation:
Cooper's Cowboy Pork Chops. Substitute 2-inch-thick double-cut bone-in pork loin chops for the sirloin. Move them to a cooler spot when they reach 125°F, and remove them from the grill at 145°F.

Goat Ropers' Barbecue

Spanish shepherds raised cattle for money, sheep for wool, and goats for meat. The herders brought this tradition along with livestock to Texas and northern Mexico. In 1765, a Spanish census counted tens of thousands of head of cattle, sheep, and goats belonging to the Spanish missions on the South Texas plains.

The Spanish *pastores*, or shepherds, adapted their style of herding to the vast distances by working on horseback. The mounted shepherds became known as *vaqueros*, which we translate as "cowboys."

After the missions were abandoned, the livestock proliferated in the wild. At the end of the Civil War, there were some three million long-horns in Texas. The early Texas cowboys who went to herd these wild cattle adopted the clothing, saddlery, and roping techniques of the vaqueros. They were called "buckaroos," a mispronunciation of *vaqueros*.

A few cowboys out "cow hunting" couldn't eat a whole longhorn, so they followed the example of the vaqueros and ate goat. An eighteen- or twenty-pound *cabrito* was just the right amount of meat for dinner, which is why goat meat has remained a favorite of cowboys to this day. Barbecued goat is a Texas culinary tradition that's now more than three centuries old.

Barbecued Goat

THE BRADY GOAT COOK-OFF, HELD EVERY YEAR over Labor Day Weekend in Brady, is a barbecue contest devoted exclusively to goat. Lonnie Rankin of Miles, Texas, and his team, Miles Messenger Messy Cookers, have won the Brady Superbowl (open only to previous winners) twice. This is Lonnie's simplified recipe, for people who want to try to barbecue goat in the backyard.

1 goat hindquarter (2½ to 3 pounds) cut into 1-inch-thick steaks

¼ cup Rankin's Spicy Dry Rub (facing page)
1 cup butter, melted

Rub the goat steaks all over with the dry rub and allow them to come to room temperature. Light an indirect fire in your barbecue with a water pan. Use wood chips, chunks, or logs, and keep up a good level of smoke. Maintain a temperature between 275° and 325°F.

Place the steaks directly over the coals until you get a nice color, turning once, then move them to indirect heat and cook, turning and brushing the steaks with the butter every 30 to 45 minutes. If the fire gets hot, turn and baste the steaks more often. The meat should be tender after 3 to 4 hours, but start tasting it before then, because if you cook it too long, it will dry out. Great barbecued goat is all a matter of timing. Serve hot.

SERVES 4 TO 6

Rankin's Spicy Dry Rub

YOU PROBABLY DON'T LIKE MSG IN YOUR FOOD, BUT YOU PROBABLY DON'T cook much goat, either. Substitute a meat tenderizer that doesn't contain MSG if you prefer.

½ cup salt

⅓ cup ground black pepper

¼ cup paprika

¼ cup chili powder

½ cup garlic powder

2 tablespoons MSG

Combine all of the ingredients in a shaker bottle, cap tightly, and shake the bottle to mix well. Store at room temperature for up to 2 months.

MAKES ABOUT 2 CUPS

FEEDING THE COTTON PICKERS

The Rise of the Barbecue Business

Cotton pickers on their way home to Mexico stop for a snack and a cold drink at a filling station. *Photo by Russell Lee*

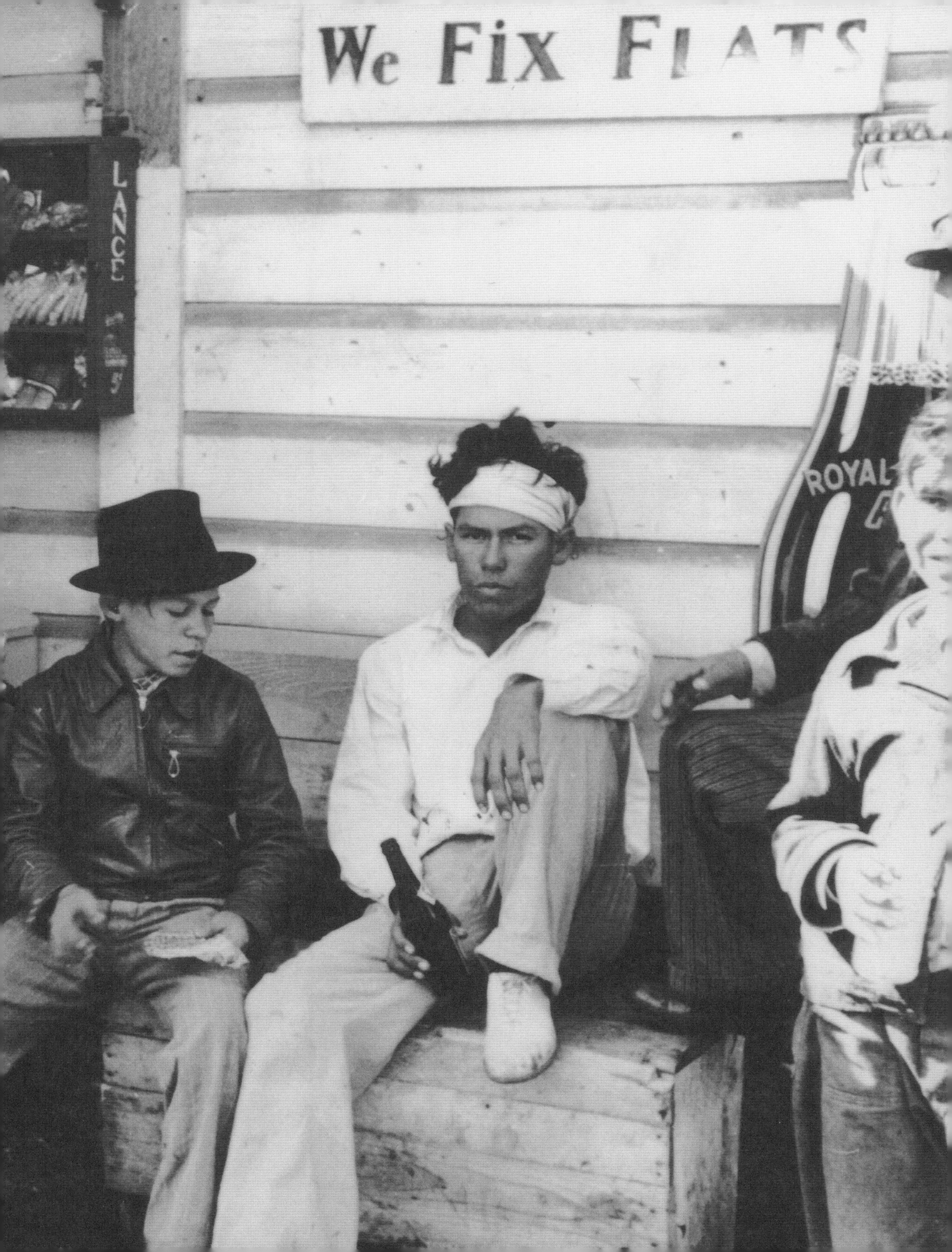
We Fix FLATS
LANCE
ROYAL

t was the cotton pickers who turned Texas barbecue into a big business. From the late 1800s until cotton picking was mechanized in the early 1960s, migrant workers picked their way across the Texas cotton belt every year, beginning in the Lower Rio Grande Valley, where cotton ripened in late June, and working their way up to Lubbock, where the cotton was ready to harvest in September. In 1938, the number of migrant workers in the state was estimated at around 600,000 people. The monumental task of feeding this army gave rise to the first generation of Texas barbecue entrepreneurs.

The pickers descended on the grocery stores and meat markets of the small towns where they worked, looking for anything that was ready to eat. Their favorites were the smoked cuts and sausages at the meat market, which they ate right off of the butcher paper with crackers, white bread, pickles, and whatever else they could find on the store's shelves.

"My daddy, William Harris Smolik, opened Smolik's Meat Market in Karnes City in 1918," remembers William Benedict "Bill" Smolik.

Cotton pickers in a field near
San Antonio, 1930.

The Long Walk

"The pickers ate barbecue at our place for breakfast, lunch, and dinner in those days. Dad used to keep the money in a bushel basket during cotton-picking season. And it was my job to count it. I remember one Saturday we made a thousand dollars in one day, selling barbecue at fifty cents a pound."

"Cotton pickers ate at the meat markets because they weren't allowed in restaurants," said Joe Capello, the manager of City Market in Luling. "They bought their meat out of the back door and then they sat on the ground in the parking lot and ate it right there."

From the end of the Civil War until the Great Depression, the pickers were mostly Hispanics. But in 1930, Herbert Hoover's secretary of labor, William N. Doak, began deporting undocumented aliens. Federal immigration authorities rounded up 82,400 Hispanics in the American Southwest and "repatriated" them to Mexico in hopes of relieving unemployment for American citizens.

For a few years during the worst of the Depression, Okies, busted farmers, and other whites joined blacks and Hispanics in the cotton fields. And in the towns near the fields where they picked cotton, the poor whites were treated with the same disdain. In his book *The White Scourge: Mexicans, Blacks, and Poor Whites in Texas Cotton Culture*, author Neil Foley explains how cotton culture made the people on the lowest rung of its economic ladder the untouchables of its caste system, regardless of skin color.

"Barbecue joints were on the wrong side of the tracks in those days," explained Vencil Mares at his bar, the Taylor Cafe. "You didn't see women or children hanging around Southside Market in Elgin. And this place was even worse. I used to break up a knife fight in here almost every night. It didn't bother me a bit in those days. I had just come back from the Normandy invasion!"

"Cotton-picking season lasted for six weeks," Edgar Black Jr., of Black's Barbecue in Lockhart, told me. Picking began in Lockhart in late July or early August and ended on September 16, Mexican Independence Day. "And all during that time there were hundreds of cotton pickers around the square every day. They started coming in the minute we opened at 7:00 A.M., and they kept coming until we closed. We served nothing but beef and sausage on butcher paper with crackers on the side. That was it. We didn't have time for anything else. Sausage was a dime, three rings for a quarter."

During the harvest season, gas stations, beer halls, and anybody with a smoker got into the barbecue business. Taylor, a cotton-shipping center, had a high concentration of barbecue joints. Louie Mueller's, which began as a grocery store, and Taylor Cafe, which opened in 1948 as a beer joint, are still two of the state's most famous.

In the 1990s, Southside Market in Elgin and Kreuz Market in Lockhart, two Texas barbecue institutions that built their reputations as rough-and-tumble joints in the days of the cotton pickers, left their original buildings and moved into pleasantly decorated new restaurants; and with those shifts, Texas barbecue began evolving into a wholesome family business. But hopefully, we will always remember our roots.

Such Texas barbecue traditions as using a sheet of butcher paper for a plate, eating without utensils, and wrapping smoked meat in plain white bread are frowned upon by polite society. Few people understand these odd practices anymore, and even fewer remember that they trace their origins to the days when the cotton pickers came to town.

The recipes in this chapter include some of the cotton pickers' old favorites, along with some modern sandwiches that recall the innovative ways in which itinerant farmworkers once turned the simplest ingredients into satisfying meals.

Vencil Mares
TAYLOR CAFE

Vencil Mares is the dean of Central Texas pitmasters. He began his barbecue career at the original location of Southside Market in downtown Elgin, where he learned how to make Elgin sausage. Mares opened the Taylor Cafe in 1948, and the place hasn't changed since then. It still has two entrances and two bars—a leftover from the days of segregation.

Vencil Mares's Bohunk Sausage

VENCIL MARES OF THE TAYLOR CAFE IN TAYLOR learned how to make sausage at Southside Market in Elgin. He started working there in 1946. This is his own sausage recipe, and since he's a Bohemian Czech, he calls it bohunk sausage.·

6 pounds boneless beef rump roast, cut into pieces or beef trimmings
4 pounds fatty pork shoulder, cut into strips
¼ cup salt
3 tablespoons coarsely ground black pepper
Vegetable oil for frying
Medium hog casings (available at butcher shops)

Grind the beef rump and pork shoulder together through the ¼-inch plate of a meat grinder (the chili plate). In a large bowl, combine the ground meat with the salt and pepper and knead the mixture with your hands until everything is well blended.

In a small skillet, heat a little vegetable oil. Form a meatball-size piece of the mixture into a small patty and fry it. Taste for seasoning and adjust as needed.

Soak the hog casings in lukewarm water. Using a sausage stuffer or a pastry bag, stuff the meat mixture into the hog casings and tie into 4- to 6-inch links. The sausage will keep refrigerated for 3 to 4 days, or frozen for up to 2 months.

When you're ready to cook the sausages, poach them in warm (140°F) water for 10 minutes or until set. Meanwhile, set up your smoker with wood chips or chunks at 275°F. Sear the links on a grate over hot coals for 3 minutes on each side, or until nicely browned. Move them to indirect heat over a drip pan and smoke for 30 minutes, or until cooked through. Serve hot.

MAKES 10 POUNDS

Vencil's Slow Beans

DON'T BE IN A RUSH TO COOK BEANS, VENCIL Mares advises. They taste best when they are cooked very slowly. A slow cooker is the perfect cooking vessel for these home-cooked pintos.

2 cups dried pinto beans

6 cups water, plus more as needed

½ onion, finely chopped

1 cup finely chopped bacon

1 tablespoon chili powder

1 teaspoon salt

1 teaspoon ground black pepper

Pick over the beans and rinse well. Transfer the beans to a slow cooker, add the remaining ingredients, and stir to mix. Cook on the high setting for 2 hours, then turn the heat to low and cook for 8 hours, or for up to overnight. The beans should be very tender. Check occasionally and add more water as needed to keep the beans covered.

Taste and adjust the seasoning. Serve hot.

MAKES ABOUT 6 CUPS; SERVES 6 TO 8

Variation:

Beans and Sausage. At the Taylor Cafe, Vencil Mares serves a bowl of these beans topped with sliced bohunk sausage (see page 182) and a little chopped onion. You can spike the beans with hot sauce, if you like. Serve the dish with lots of saltines.

Elgin Hot Guts

There's a bottle of hot-pepper sauce on the table at almost every old meat market—even the ones that refuse to serve barbecue sauce. Lots of people wonder why. "It's to heat up the sausage," Bryan Bracewell, a third-generation barbecue man, explains.

The most famous barbecue sausage in Texas is Elgin (pronounced with a soft *g*) sausage, or "Elgin hot guts," as the old-timers called it. This spicy sausage originated at the Southside Market, one of the oldest barbecue operations in the state. The original meat market in downtown Elgin opened in 1886. In 1992, Southside moved to a larger, cleaner location out on the highway. The kitchen also toned down the spiciness of the sausage.

"Elgin hot guts were really spicy. We wanted to appeal to families," Bryan Bracewell says. "So over the years, we've cut way back on the cayenne." Texas barbecue sausage isn't as hot as it used to be in the good ol' days.

And that's why you'll find a bottle of hot sauce on every table.

Cecil Sanchez and the Bohemian Special

"Half Mexican, half German" is the way Cecil Sanchez describes his ancestry. Cecil is the pitmaster at the Mustang Creek BBQ in Louise. It's a rural gas station, convenience store, and barbecue joint in the Czech enclave south of El Campo. Bottles of homemade sauerkraut for sale are lined up next to the cash register.

The first time I stopped by, I noticed Cecil carving up the fatty point of a juicy, black barbecued brisket. I started to order the sliced brisket, but then I saw the signature sandwich on the overhead plastic menu board: Bohemian Special.

It turned out to be a sliced brisket sandwich topped with barbecued Czech sausage. No, the sausage is not made in-house, Cecil told me. The links came from Prasek's Hillje Smokehouse, a legendary meat market and former feed store and saloon in the little Czech community of Hillje three miles north on Highway 59. (You can mail order the sausages at www.praseks.com.)

After I placed my order, I hovered over the butcher block to ensure that my sandwich was made from the fatty pieces that had just hit the cutting board. I ate the sandwich in the parking lot.

Mustang Creek's Bohemian Special

THIS RECIPE ASSUMES YOU HAVE SOME magnificent barbecued brisket and hot smoked Czech sausage on hand.

1 large hamburger bun or kaiser roll, split and toasted
¼ cup barbecue sauce of your choice
8 ounces barbecued brisket from the fatty point thinly sliced
Salt and ground black pepper
1 link Czech sausage, barbecued and quartered or sliced lengthwise
1 large onion slice
5 pickle chips

Spread the cut sides of the toasted bun with the barbecue sauce and place the bottom half, cut-side up, on a plate. Arrange the brisket slices on the bottom of the bun and season with salt and pepper. Layer the sausage over the brisket, center the onion slice on top, and then spread the pickle chips over the onion. Close the sandwich with the bun top, and serve.

To make the sandwich easier to eat, wrap it in white sandwich paper or wax paper to hold the bun together.

MAKES 1 SANDWICH

Railhead's Barbecued Bologna Sandwiches

I THOUGHT THIS SOUNDED LIKE A HORRIBLE idea until I tried it. Barbecued bologna on a bun tastes like barbecued hot dogs. At the Railhead Smokehouse in Fort Worth, these sandwiches are served with french fries and cold beer.

One 1-pound whole bologna (large size)

4 hamburger buns, split and toasted

Barbecue sauce of your choice

½ cup chopped onion

8 slices dill pickle

Set up your smoker for indirect heat with a water pan. Use wood chips, chunks, or logs, and keep up a good level of smoke. Maintain a temperature between 250° and 300°F.

Smoke the bologna for 1 hour over indirect heat. It should have a little char on the edges and swell until it is about to burst.

Spread the cut sides of the toasted buns with the barbecue sauce and place the bottom half of each bun, cut-side up, on a plate. Cut the bologna into four thick slices, and place one slice on each bun bottom. Top with the onion and pickle slices, dividing them evenly, then serve immediately.

MAKES 4 SANDWICHES

The smoked beef oozed buttery-tasting tallow. The Prasek's coarse-ground beef-and-pork sausage was seasoned with a lot of black pepper. The raw onion, pickles, and barbecue sauce were a fine complement. In 2008, I declared Mustang Creek BBQ's Bohemian Special a masterpiece, and told anyone who would listen all about it.

In the last few years, barbecue joints around the state have come up with their own spins on the brisket and sausage sandwich that Cecil Sanchez created in his humble gas station–barbecue joint in rural Louise. In fact, nowadays it's hard to find a barbecue joint in Texas that *doesn't* sell a brisket and sausage sandwich.

I'm not sure what Cecil thinks about that, but I say, "the more the merrier."

How to Eat Sausage

The cotton pickers' habit of eating smoked meat with whatever they could find on the shelves of a grocery store gave us the practice of making sandwiches out of white bread, tortillas, hamburger buns, and crackers. Here are a few quick tips for making barbecued sausage sandwiches.

Sausage Wrap

Wrap a flour tortilla or a slice of white bread around a link of barbecued sausage. Spread a little barbecue sauce on the sausage and sprinkle with chopped onion, if desired.

Sausage Crackers

Slice a sausage into rounds and put each slice on a saltine. Sprinkle with Louisiana hot sauce and top with a 1-inch square of onion.

Sausage on a Bun

Cut a sausage link in half crosswise, and then slice the sausage halves lengthwise. Split a hamburger bun or kaiser roll, toast the halves, and spread the cut side of each half with the barbecue sauce of your choice. Line up the sausage slices on the bottom of the bun, top with pickles and onion, and close with the bun top.

Black's Simple Slaw

WHEN BLACK'S BARBECUE IN LOCKHART finally decided to start serving side dishes, the staff vowed to keep them as simple as possible. Here's the kitchen's easy recipe for coleslaw.

½ cup olive oil	1 teaspoon celery salt
¼ cup distilled white vinegar	1 teaspoon sugar
1 teaspoon salt	1 teaspoon prepared
1 teaspoon ground black	mustard
pepper	1 head green cabbage,
1 teaspoon celery seeds	cored and shredded

In a small bowl, stir together the olive oil, vinegar, salt, pepper, celery seeds, celery salt, sugar, and mustard, mixing well. Put the cabbage in a large bowl, add the oil mixture, and stir and toss until well mixed. Cover and allow to mellow in the refrigerator overnight before serving.

MAKES ABOUT 8 CUPS; SERVES 6 TO 8

Laura Novosad's Confetti Slaw

"I CAN'T STAND SWEET COLESLAW," LAURA Novosad told me. "So I came up with this recipe. It looks real pretty with all the colors. Beans and coleslaw have gone over pretty well here at Novosad's. But we still get a lot of requests for canned peaches." Serve this slaw with any kind of barbecue—and with canned peaches.

1 head green cabbage, cored
½ head red cabbage, cored
3 large carrots, peeled
1 cup Wish-Bone Italian dressing or the Italian dressing of your choice

Shred both cabbages and the carrots and combine in a large bowl. Add the Italian dressing and toss and stir to mix well. Allow to marinate for 1 hour before serving.

MAKES ABOUT 8 CUPS; SERVES 6 TO 8

LEGENDS

A Woman at Novosad's Market

"My granddad started barbecuing in Taylor. He sold his place there to Rudy Mikeska and moved here in 1959," Nathan Novosad said from behind the counter of Novosad's Market in Hallettsville. Novosad is a Czech name, and Hallettsville is a Czech town. "My dad served barbecue on butcher paper without any sides, but when my wife, Laura, got into the business, we started making beans and slaw."

"I freaked people out when I began working here," Laura giggled. "First a woman and then side dishes." Cold canned peaches were the only side dish served with smoked meat before Laura took over. "It's a tradition around here to eat cold canned peaches with barbecue in the summer. I tried to switch from peaches in heavy syrup to fancy homemade ones, but everybody got upset," Laura remembers.

"Some things you just can't change."

TENDER BONES

Urban Rib Joints

The late Bobby Lewis served up barbecue and the blues at his now-shuttered Third Ward nightclub, Miss Ann's Playpen.

fter the Emancipation Proclamation was signed, African-Americans from East Texas and the rest of the South gravitated to large cities. In every city of size, they established at least one outpost of Southern-style barbecue. Many of these black urban barbecue joints were justly famous for their ribs. A few of them became legendary institutions that were considered treasures by their hometowns.

Miller's in San Antonio was one of the best-loved barbecue joints in the state for many years. Founder Harvey Miller grew up in the farm town of Floresville. He started Miller's Bar-B-Q in the back of his house in San Antonio in 1941, selling barbecue sandwiches for fifteen cents apiece, plates for a quarter. His daughters, Myrtle and Bernice, kept the business going until 1990. Miller's Bar-B-Q was never listed in the yellow pages and never advertised, but it attracted all races, classes, and age groups to an obscure suburban backyard for fifty years. The *Washington Post*, *Texas Monthly*, and other publications took note.

Myrtle Miller Johnson serving ribs in 1990. Myrtle ordered that Miller's Bar-B-Q in San Antonio be torn down upon her death so that no one could give the family a bad name with inferior barbecue.

The business operated in violation of zoning and health department regulations, but the inspectors told the Millers that the barbecue joint was too important to the city of San Antonio to write any citations. The Millers were famous for their ribs and for their secret-recipe barbecue sauce. "Everybody wants the secret of my famous barbecue sauce," Myrtle told an interviewer in 1990 when the place closed. "People have offered to buy the recipe, and I've never been tempted to sell it. We worked on it together, Mama, Daddy, and me."

Myrtle Miller Johnson died in 1999 at the age of ninety-six. She took the barbecue sauce recipe to her grave.

Sam's on East 12th Street in Austin was a favorite of blues guitarist Stevie Ray Vaughan and is still popular with the late-night music crowd. Unlike the old meat markets out in the country, which often sell out at noon and close up before five, urban barbecue joints like Sam's are hopping at three o'clock in the morning. Sam Mays, who was born in Round Rock, opened Sam's in 1978. Son Willie and daughter Wanda are in charge these days. When Sam's burned down in 1993, the entire community pitched in to rebuild the place. Volunteers donated time, money, and materials with no strings attached—just to keep Sam's in business.

The barbecue joint called Pizzitola's on Shepherd Drive in Houston traces its history back to the 1930s, when it was known as Shepherd Drive Bar-B-Q. It was opened by John Davis and his wife, Leila. In the era of segregation, it was a blacks-only restaurant. Legend has it that the barbecue was so good, white River Oaks residents bought ribs to go out of the back door and ate at cable-spool tables in the parking lot.

When John Davis passed away in the early 1980s, the family wasn't interested in running the restaurant. But life-long barbecue buff Jerry Pizzitola, who had been eating there for years, couldn't bear to see the place go out of business, so he offered to lease the restaurant from the family. The original wood-fired brick pits, which are the oldest in Houston, were grandfathered under the lease arrangement. The restaurant still serves two-and-a-half-pound slabs of spareribs seasoned with nothing but salt and pepper. They are amazingly crispy.

Everybody cooks ribs these days, and all kinds of techniques come in and out of style. But we can thank legendary black barbecue men like Harvey Miller, Sam Mays, and John Davis for making smoky "bones" such a big deal in Texas.

PEPSI

SAM'S BBQ.
Serving
Austins Original Hot Sausage

SA
BA

Wanda Mays and friends in front of
Sam's BBQ in Austin.

Falls County Easy Pork Ribs

ROCKNEY TERRY (SEE PAGE 76) GAVE ME THIS EASY RECIPE FOR PORK RIBS. Wrapping the ribs in aluminum foil after a couple of hours of smoking is a quick way to produce the falling-apart texture. Terry likes his ribs without sauce. "It's like a good steak. Who needs sauce?" he says.

1 tablespoon salt

1 tablespoon coarsely ground black pepper

1 tablespoon sugar

1 teaspoon garlic powder

1 rack 3½ and down pork spareribs

Barbecue sauce of your choice (optional)

Combine the salt, pepper, sugar, and garlic powder in a shaker bottle and shake to mix well. Pat the ribs dry, then season them all over with the seasoning mix and rub it into the meat.

Set up your smoker for indirect heat. Use wood chips, chunks, or logs, and keep up a good level of smoke. Maintain a temperature between 250° and 300°F.

Place the ribs, bone-side down, in the smoker as far away from the fire as possible. Cook for 2 to 2½ hours, or until the ribs are a nice color.

Remove the rack from the smoker and wrap the ribs in aluminum foil. Return the ribs to the smoker and continue to cook for 1 hour longer, or until the ribs are falling-apart tender. Serve hot with barbecue sauce, if desired.

SERVES 2 TO 4

Variation:
4 and Ups. This recipe will also work well on larger rib racks, but you'll need to increase the cooking time to 3½ to 4 hours on the smoker and to about 2 hours in the foil.

PORK RIB TERMINOLOGY

3½ and down: *Most Texas barbecue joints and all top cook-off competitors insist on 3½ and down pork spareribs. This is a meat industry classification that refers to the weight of the ribs (under 3½ pounds). Due to the increasing demand for ribs, these choice spareribs are getting harder and harder to find.*

To get your hands on some 3½ and down ribs, you'll need to find a real butcher. Don't confuse the average meat-counter attendant at the supermarket with a butcher. When I asked for 3½ and down ribs at one super-market, the guy behind the scales offered to cut a 5-pound slab in half! Discount stores sometimes sell 3½ and down ribs in cases and three-packs. But your best bet is to order them from a quality meat market or the head butcher at a good grocery store.

Baby back ribs: *These are the very tender but very expensive under-2-pound racks of ribs. They are favored in grilling recipes because they cook very quickly. You can substitute baby backs for 3½ and downs in any of these recipes. Just decrease the cooking time a little.*

4 and up: *These giant racks of ribs (4 pounds and up) come from larger hogs and are not the best for barbecuing. You will find*
5- *and even 6-pound racks in grocery stores these days. Even the 3½ and down ribs sold in many meat markets are actually larger ribs that have been cut down to a lower weight. But a 5-pound rack that has been cut down to 3½ pounds doesn't cook the same as a rack from a smaller pig that weighed 3½ pounds to begin with.*

Cook-off competitors have devised some elaborate techniques to get these giant racks tender. Be sure to leave yourself 6 to 7 hours to cook this size.

St. Louis cut: *To trim a rack of ribs St. Louis style, you cut off the breastbone, back flap, and lower ribs to produce a squared-up rack that fits nicely on the grill. The breastbone is connected to the top few ribs; it runs north and south while the ribs run east and west. Removing the breastbone also makes carving at the table much easier.*

Skinning your ribs: *There is a membrane on the bone side of a rack of ribs that many barbecuers like to remove. Some argue that this process speeds cooking time; some say it makes the ribs more tender. When cooking 4 and ups with a braising liquid, it is definitely a good idea to remove the membrane, so that the steam can more easily penetrate the meat.*

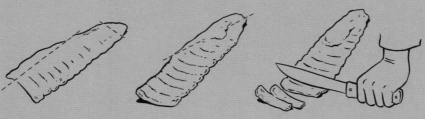

Trim breastbone and lower ribs

Cut off the back flap and remove the skin if desired

Carve the ribs

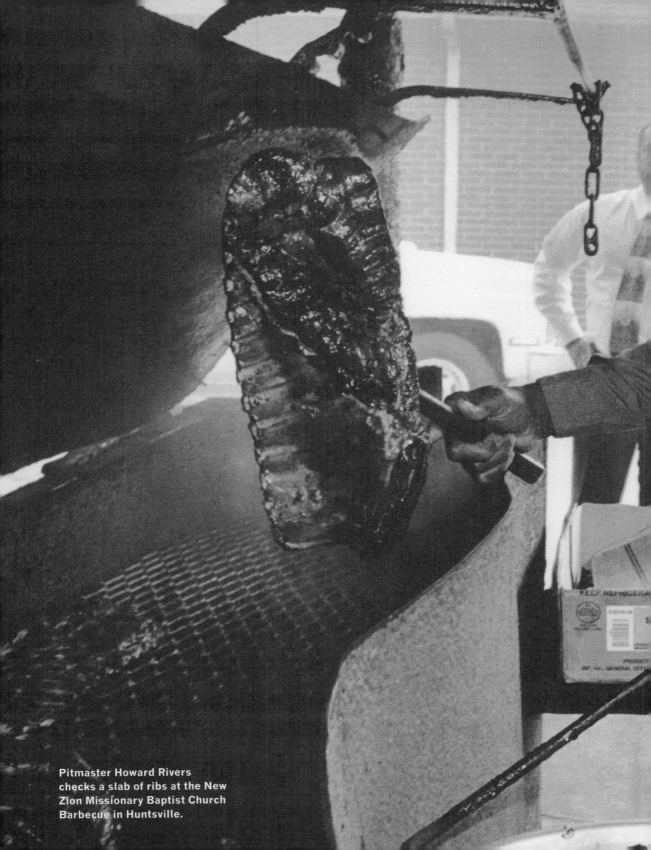

Pitmaster Howard Rivers checks a slab of ribs at the New Zion Missionary Baptist Church Barbecue in Huntsville.

Cook 3½ and down pork ribs until the bones protrude and the rack is just about to fall apart.

New Zion Missionary Baptist Church Barbecue

Howard Rivers lifts the lid of the steel barbecue pit and sticks a huge fork into a slab of ribs. You know when they're done because the fork slides through easy, he tells me.

Sitting around, shooting the breeze with the guys on the front porch of the New Zion Missionary Baptist Church Barbecue in Huntsville looks like a fine way to spend the afternoon. The scene reminds me more of a barbecue in my backyard than the hustle and bustle of a restaurant (except that there isn't any beer). I pull up a chair and join a conversation about this year's pecan harvest. Barbecue may not actually be a religion in Texas, but the two institutions are closely associated.

East Texas camp meetings put on by traveling preachers always featured free barbecue. The sponsors of the meeting would donate sheep, goats, and cattle, and the smell of the meat cooking would attract "joiners" from all around. The preaching, testifying, and singing of hymns would continue for as long as the barbecue held out.

The Texas camp meeting, barbecue style, is still going strong here at Mount Zion Missionary Baptist. Sitting down with the congregation in the funky little church hall is an experience every true barbecue believer should have at least once. It's like a pilgrimage to Mecca—only with pork.

New Zion Ribs

AT NEW ZION MISSIONARY BAPTIST CHURCH Barbecue in Huntsville, ribs are cooked on the smoker for three hours and then held, a dozen racks at a time, in a large ice chest. The ice chest keeps the ribs hot and traps the steam so they become more tender. You can accomplish the same thing by dousing the ribs with barbecue sauce and wrapping them in aluminum foil.

1 rack 3½ and down pork spareribs
TexJoy Bar-B-Q Seasoning or dry rub of your choice
Barbecue sauce of your choice, heated

Season the ribs on both sides with the dry rub, wrap them in plastic wrap, and put them in the refrigerator overnight.

Set up your smoker for indirect heat. Use wood chips, chunks, or logs, and keep up a good level of smoke. Maintain a temperature between 250° and 300°F.

Place the ribs, bone-side down, on the smoker as far away from the fire as possible. Cook for 3 to 3½ hours, turning the ribs every hour for the first 2 hours and then every 30 minutes.

Remove the ribs from the smoker and cut the rack in half crosswise. Brush both halves on both sides with the heated barbecue sauce—do not use cold sauce!—and wrap them in aluminum foil. Return the ribs to the smoker (or place in a 250°F oven) for 15 to 30 minutes, or until they're falling-apart tender.

Remove the ribs from the smoker, unwrap and carve the ribs between the bones, pile onto a platter, and serve hot with extra sauce on the side.

SERVES 2 TO 4

The barbecue began in 1981 when Sister Ward cooked some barbecue to feed volunteers who were painting the church. The barbecue stopped traffic, as passing motorists begged to buy some freshly cooked ribs for dinner. Selling barbecue was so lucrative, the church did it again a week later, and pretty soon it became a permanent activity every Wednesday through Saturday. The down-home cooking and good-hearted volunteers make this a wonderful scene. It may not be enough to convert you, but I would gladly sit through a three-hour sermon if I knew this kind of homemade barbecue was waiting for me at the end.

Art Blondin's Chipotle-Marinated Ribs

COOK-OFF COMPETITOR AND BARBECUE-JOINT OWNER ART BLONDIN WAS A rib specialist. At Artz Rib House in Austin, he served every size and shape of ribs imaginable. After Artz Rib House closed, Art Blondin opened a place in Florence called Art's Ribs & BBQ. Here's his favorite recipe for baby back ribs.

ART'S CHIPOTLE MARINADE
¼ cup red wine
¼ cup honey
¼ cup Búfalo chipotle sauce or Chipotle
   Ketchup (page 111)

¼ cup canola oil
Salt and ground black pepper

1 rack baby back ribs
Sweet Pork Rub (facing page)

To make the marinade: In a small bowl, stir together the wine, honey, chipotle sauce, and canola oil. Season with salt and pepper, mixing well.

Put the ribs into a resealable plastic freezer bag, add the marinade, seal closed, and turn the bag as needed to coat the ribs evenly. Or, put the ribs in a flat plastic container, add the marinade, turn the ribs as needed to coat evenly, and seal the container closed. (It is okay to cut the rack in half crosswise so the ribs will fit in the bag or container.) Marinate the ribs at room temperature for 1 to 2 hours, or in the refrigerator overnight.

Set up your smoker for indirect heat. Use wood chips, chunks, or logs, and keep up a good level of smoke. Maintain a temperature between 200° and 225°F.

Remove the ribs from the marinade and sprinkle them all over with the rub, pressing it into the meat. Allow the ribs to dry.

Place the ribs, bone-side down, in the smoker as far away from the fire as possible. Cook for 3 to 3½ hours, or until a toothpick inserted between the bones goes through easily. Cut the ribs apart between the bones, pile on a platter, and serve hot.

SERVES 2 OR 3

Sweet Pork Rub

BROWN SUGAR MAKES A PORK RUB TASTY, BUT IT ALSO REQUIRES VERY LOW temperatures to prevent the rub from burning.

¼ cup kosher salt

¼ cup chili powder

2 tablespoons dark brown sugar

2 tablespoons coarsely ground
   black pepper

2 tablespoons garlic powder

2 tablespoons onion powder

1 tablespoon sweet Hungarian paprika

In a small bowl, stir together all of the ingredients, mixing well. Store the rub in a tightly capped shaker jar or a regular jar. It will keep in a cool cupboard for up to 2 months.

MAKES ABOUT 1 CUP

Rosemary Broasted Big Ribs

HERE, BROASTING, WHICH COMBINES BRAISING AND ROASTING, IS USED
to cook a large rack of ribs. You can also use a marinade as the braising liquid to
tenderize tough 4 and ups before smoking.

1 rack 4 and up pork spareribs

1 cup red wine

1 cup water

3 large sprigs rosemary

5 garlic cloves, crushed

Salt and freshly ground black pepper

Bourbon Glaze (facing page; optional)

Preheat the oven to 350°F.

Trim the rib rack St. Louis style and remove the membrane (see page 197).
In a roasting pan large enough to accommodate the rack, combine the wine, water,
rosemary, and garlic, mixing well. Arrange the rack, bone-side down, over the herbs.
Sprinkle the meat with salt and pepper. The top of the ribs should be above the
liquid so they steam rather than boil. Cover the pan with foil.

Bake for 3 to 4 hours, or until a toothpick inserted between the bones goes
through easily.

Meanwhile, set up your smoker for indirect heat with a water pan. Use wood
chips, chunks, or logs, and keep up a good level of smoke. Maintain a temperature
between 225° and 275°F.

When the ribs are ready, remove the rack from the roasting pan and apply the
glaze to the meat side with a spoon or brush, if desired. Place the rack, bone-side
down, in the smoker as far away from the fire as possible. Cook for about 1 hour,
or until the glaze bubbles. Be careful; it burns easily.

Remove the rack from the smoker, cut the ribs apart between the bones, pile on a
platter, and serve hot.

SERVES 3 OR 4

Bourbon Glaze

THIS IS A FAVORITE RIB GLAZE FROM THE JACK DANIEL'S COOK-OFF.

1 shot bourbon

1 shot cider vinegar

½ cup honey

1 teaspoon Dijon mustard

1 teaspoon butter

In a small saucepan, combine all of the ingredients over medium heat and heat, stirring occasionally, until the butter melts and the ingredients are thoroughly combined.

Remove from the heat and use immediately, applying the glaze with a heat-resistant basting brush.

MAKES ABOUT ¾ CUP

Lyndon B. Johnson and Hubert Humphrey dig in to the ribs at a victory celebration on the LBJ Ranch in 1964.

Oversize 3-2-1 Ribs

THE NUMBERS REFER TO THE SUGGESTED COOKING TIMES: 3 HOURS OF smoking, 2 hours of braising in a foil pan, and 1 hour of glazing. This is a recipe for a big rack of ribs that takes forever to cook. Don't use it for baby backs or 3½ and down spareribs or you will end up with a pile of mushy bones. Use Jalapeño Rib Glaze (facing page) or another of the Favorite Glazes (page 85).

1 rack 4 and up pork spareribs

1 cup cider vinegar or cane vinegar

3 tablespoons Sweet Pork Rub (page 205), plus more for finishing

1 cup Dr Pepper

3 garlic cloves, crushed

Glaze of your choice

Trim the rib rack St. Louis style and remove the membrane (see page 197). In a roasting pan, rinse both sides of the rack with the vinegar and then allow the rack to soak for 15 minutes.

Remove the rack from the pan, shaking off the vinegar, and discard the vinegar in the pan. Sprinkle the rack on both sides with the rub and press it into the meat. Wrap the rack in plastic wrap and marinate in the refrigerator for several hours.

Set up your smoker for indirect heat with a water pan. Start a fire with charcoal briquettes and add hardwood lump charcoal or hardwood logs or chunks. Maintain a temperature between 250° and 275°F.

Place the rack, bone-side down, in the smoker as far away from the fire as possible. Cook the ribs, turning them every 15 minutes so they cook evenly, for about 3 hours. The ribs should be well browned.

Remove the rack from the smoker and place it, bone-side down, in an aluminum foil pan. Add the Dr Pepper and garlic and cover the pan tightly with aluminum foil. Place the foil pan in the smoker and cook the ribs, undisturbed, for 2 hours.

After 2 hours, check to see if the ribs are ready by inserting a toothpick between the bones. If the toothpick goes through easily, the ribs are ready. If not, re-cover the pan and cook for another 20 minutes, or until the ribs are very tender.

When the ribs are tender, transfer them to the grill meat-side up and apply the glaze with a spoon or brush. Shake a little extra rub over the sticky glaze, then cook the rack over low heat (about 225°F) for about 1 hour, or until the glaze begins to set. The glaze burns easily, so make sure the fire is not too hot.

Remove the rack from the grill, cut the ribs apart between the bones, fan on a platter, and serve hot.

SERVES 3 OR 4

Jalapeño Rib Glaze

IF YOU'RE COOKING A WHOLE LOT OF RIBS, HERE'S A LARGE-BATCH RECIPE for a homemade chile glaze that tastes even better than the kind you make from jalapeño jelly.

4 jalapeño chiles, seeded and chopped
1 cup diced red bell pepper
2 cups cane vinegar or cider vinegar

4 cups sugar
¾ cup liquid pectin

In a nonreactive saucepan, combine the chiles, bell pepper, vinegar, and sugar over high heat and bring to a boil, stirring to dissolve the sugar. Turn the heat to low and simmer, stirring often, for 20 minutes. Be careful that the mixture does not boil over.

Remove the pan from the heat and gradually add the pectin while stirring constantly. Return the pan to high heat and heat until the mixture returns to a boil. Remove the pan from the heat, pour into a heatproof bowl, and let cool.

Use the glaze immediately, or transfer to one or more airtight containers and store in the refrigerator for up to 2 weeks.

MAKES ABOUT 3 CUPS

'Regulars

After you trim your pork ribs, cook the trimmings separately. First of all, it would be a crime to throw away all that meat, and second, it's an old East Texas tradition. The breastbone, back flap, and bottom pieces were cooked by themselves and set aside at barbecue joints like Burney's in Houston's Third Ward. These odd scraps of cooked meat were known as 'regulars. (The term is probably a corruption of the word irregulars.)

At Burney's, people would come to the back door and the barbecue crew would sell them the burnt ends and crispy trimmings from the ribs, Karen Mayberry, Joe Burney's daughter, remembers. "They called them the 'regulars. Some people wanted them because they were too poor to buy a whole plate of barbecue, but lots of people liked them just because they tasted so good." Only people who have been eating barbecue for a long time know to ask for 'regulars.

When you barbecue ribs at home, make yourself a special "cook's treat." Trim the ribs, season the scraps with rib rub, and smoke the trimmings along with the ribs. The 'regulars will be done much more quickly than the rest of the rack, so you'll have something to munch on while you're cooking.

East Texas Rib Sandwiches

ONLY VERY TENDER EAST TEXAS–STYLE RIBS ARE soft enough to make sandwiches.

1 rack well-cooked East
   Texas ribs
4 or 5 hamburger buns, split
1 cup barbecue sauce
   of your choice, heated

Onion slices for topping
Pickle slices for topping

Cut the rack into individual ribs. Dip the cut side of each bun bottom in the barbecue sauce. Place two or three ribs on each bun bottom and top with onion slices and pickle slices. Dip the cut side of each bun top in the barbecue sauce and close the sandwiches with the tops.

To eat a sandwich, just pull the protruding bones out from the falling-apart-tender meat.

MAKES 4 OR 5 SANDWICHES

Boudin-Stuffed Pork Chops

GREGORY CARTER RUNS A BARBECUE TRAILER CALLED BAR-B-QUE DONE Right in Houston's Fifth Ward. Along with brisket, ribs, and sausage, he barbecues some tasty mains like these incredible stuffed pork chops. These are a great extra to throw on the smoker when you are smoking something else.

2 bone-in, double-thick pork loin chops (about 1 pound each)

1 link Cajun boudin (about 8 ounces)
½ cup Sweet Pork Rub (page 205)

Set up your smoker for indirect heat. Use wood chips, chunks, or logs, and keep up a good level of smoke. Maintain a temperature between 225° and 275°F.

Insert a sharp knife into the side of the meaty part of the pork chop all the way to the bone, and then carefully cut horizontally in each direction to create a cavity for the stuffing. Squeeze the boudin out of its casing, divide the sausage in half, and stuff half of it into the pocket in each pork chop. Sprinkle both sides of each chop with the rub, pressing it into the meat. Coat the chops lightly with nonstick cooking spray so the meat won't stick to the grill.

Place the chops in the smoker directly over the fire and sear briefly on both sides to make good-looking grill marks. Move the chops away from the coals and close the lid. Cook the chops for about 2 hours, or until an instant-read thermometer inserted into the center of a chop away from the stuffing and bone registers 145°F for medium.

Let the chops rest for 10 minutes before serving.

SERVES 2 TO 4

BARBACOA AND BORRACHO BEANS

Down in South Texas

Armando Vera and his father cook barbacoa (cows' heads) the old-fashioned way: in a brick pit at Vera's Backyard Bar-B-Que in Brownsville.

oday, a large percentage of the state's top pitmasters are Tejanos, or Mexican-Texans. You'll find the same brisket, ribs, and sausage in Tejano barbecue joints that you'll find in the rest of the state, but there is one kind of legendary Texas barbecue that is uniquely Tejano: barbacoa.

In Central Mexico, barbacoa is usually lamb or goat meat wrapped in maguey leaves and roasted on hot coals, but it means something different in Texas. On the cattle ranches along the Mexican border, Mexican ranch hands were given part of their pay in less desirable cuts of beef, such as the head and offal. The Mexican vaqueros adapted the interior Mexican style of barbacoa to roast the cows' heads. They wrapped the heads in maguey leaves or later in aluminum foil and canvas and buried them in earthen pits lined with hot coals (*pozos* in Spanish).

Barbacoa is still a popular tradition in Texas, but the cooking methods have changed. There are reportedly two or three restaurants in the state that have been granted grandfather status by a county health department for their old barbacoa pits, but the practice won't last much longer.

"No, we don't cook it in the ground anymore," Paula Luna told me one Sunday morning at (the now-closed) Johnny's Bar-B-Q Pit in Pharr, down in the Lower Rio Grande Valley. "The health department won't let us. But I grew up in Los Ebanos, and we still do it that way down there for our family." Los Ebanos ("ebony trees" in Spanish) is a tiny border town famous for having the last rope-pulled ferry across the Rio Grande.

For her family in Los Ebanos, Paula seasons the cows' heads, or *cabezas,* with salt and pepper and then wraps them in foil. She puts each wrapped head in an empty ten-gallon metal lard container and puts the lid on it. Paula's brother buries the cans under a layer of dirt and builds a big fire on top. "You have to pack the earth down good. If you leave any air in there, it won't get done," she says. The fire burns through the night, and the cabezas are dug up in the morning.

At Johnny's Bar-B-Q Pit, Johnny Harper cooked his cabezas in a pit over a water bath. "You put the heads on a screen above the water and let them steam overnight," he told me. In the rest of Texas, *barbacoa de cabeza* is made in a conventional oven with a water bath (called a *baño María* in Spanish) underneath the head. But in the vast majority of modern Mexican restaurants that list barbacoa on the menu, the meat is actually just braised beef cheeks.

I asked Johnny and Paula how to make real barbacoa de cabeza at home. "Use an electric roaster oven," Paula told me. "You know, the kind you cook turkeys in. You put some water in the bottom and cook the head for about twelve hours—it stays real juicy."

Cook-off competitor Ernest Servantes has his own method for re-creating old-fashioned barbacoa. He seasons and smokes the heads for a while, then wraps them in foil and leaves them on the grill over a slow fire overnight.

If you have a weak stomach, I recommend you skip the recipes for barbacoa and *lengua* that follow. Skim ahead to the wonderful recipe for BBQ Pork and Garlicky Guacamole Sandwiches (page 226) and the definitive recipe for slow-cooked Borracho Beans (page 229). If you aren't easily grossed out and you really want to cook authentic barbacoa de cabeza at home, you'll find all the gory details on the pages that follow.

Three Ways to Make Barbacoa

PAULA'S BARBACOA IS LIKE THE KIND YOU GET IN A RESTAURANT—MADE without any smoke in a braising liquid. It comes out very moist with extra cooking juice to keep it wet. Cook-off competitor Ernest Servantes grew up in Uvalde, and his barbacoa is old school. It's cooked in a barbecue smoker with mesquite smoke and no liquid, so you need to have plenty of salsa on hand. My version falls somewhere between the two.

If you live in Texas, you can usually get a cow's head at any Fiesta supermarket. Get the smallest one you can find. The biggest ones don't fit in barbecue smokers, conventional ovens, or electric roaster ovens. If you don't live in Texas, see page 289 for information on ordering cows' heads.

1 cow's head, the smallest available, skinned and cleaned
Salt and ground black pepper
Garlic powder for sprinkling
Chili powder for sprinkling
2 onions, halved

Fresh corn tortillas, lime quarters, chopped onion, and fresh cilantro sprigs for serving
Pico de Gallo (page 113) or salsa picante of your choice for serving

Rinse the cow's head carefully inside and out, then cut out the tongue and reserve it for making the Lengua (Tongue) on page 224. Sprinkle salt, pepper, garlic powder, and chili powder (or your own favorite spice blend) all over the head. Proceed with one of the following methods.

PAULA'S TURKEY ROASTER OVEN BARBACOA

Put the seasoned cow's head upside down (forehead down) in an 18-quart electric roaster oven. (If it doesn't fit, trim the nose with a meat cleaver.) Add 8 cups water, put the onions in the water, and cover the oven. (If the lid won't fit, make an aluminum foil tent as described in Robb's Foil Pan Barbacoa, following.)

Turn the roaster oven to 350°F and heat for 1 hour, or until the water is boiling vigorously. Turn the heat to 250°F and allow the head to steam overnight (12 hours), or until the cheek meat easily pulls away from the bone.

ROBB'S FOIL PAN BARBACOA

Light a fire in a smoker large enough to hold the cow's head (a Big Ugly Barrel works great for this). Maintain a temperature between 225° and 250°F, and add oak or pecan wood to create some smoke. Put the seasoned cow's head forehead up in the smoker and smoke for 1½ to 2 hours, or until slightly browned.

Wearing fireproof gloves, remove the cow's head from the smoker and place it, upside down (forehead down), in an oval aluminum-foil roasting pan designed to hold a turkey. (If it doesn't fit, trim the nose with a meat cleaver.) Add 6 cups water and the onions to the bottom of the pan. Cut two sheets of heavy-duty 18-inch-wide aluminum foil long enough to cover the top of the pan with plenty to spare. Combine the two sheets by overlapping and folding them to make one 32-inch-wide piece of foil, and seal the roasting pan closed with the foil by tucking and folding it around the outside of the pan.

Place the pan in the smoker and cook the head at a temperature between 225° and 250°F overnight (12 hours), or until the cheek meat easily pulls away from the bone.

Alternatively, put the foil-wrapped pan in a 250°F oven and cook overnight (12 hours), or until the cheek meat easily pulls away from the bone. (The aluminum foil pan will be very heavy and quite flimsy. Slide it onto a cutting board to carry it into the house—and be careful!)

ERNEST SERVANTES' MESQUITE-SMOKED BARBACOA

Light a fire in a smoker large enough to hold the cow's head (a Big Ugly Barrel works great for this) and set up a water pan. Maintain a temperature between 225° and 250°F and add mesquite wood for a South Texas–style smoke flavor. Put the seasoned cow's head forehead up in the smoker and smoke for 1½ to 2 hours, or until slightly browned.

Wearing fireproof gloves, remove the head from the smoker, wrap it in heavy-duty aluminum foil with the onions, and seal tightly. Return it to the smoker and cook at a temperature between 225° and 250°F overnight (12 hours), or until the cheek meat easily pulls away from the bone.

When the cow's head is done, pull the cheek meat off, then remove the jaw bones. You'll find another large piece of meat inside. Remove any other nice chunks of meat you can find.

Cut away any excess fat, blackened meat, and cartilage, but don't clean the meat too thoroughly. The little bits of fat and gelatinized collagen are what give barbacoa its distinctive velvety texture. Chop the meat and put it in a bowl. You should end up with about 2 pounds of meat. Moisten with some cooking liquid if you have any left over.

Serve immediately with tortillas, lime quarters, chopped onion, cilantro, and pico de gallo.

SERVES 6 TO 8

Gerardo's Barbacoa de Borrego

BORREGO MEANS "LAMB," BUT AT GERARDO'S DRIVE-IN IN HOUSTON, THE kitchen crew uses a mixture of half lamb and half goat and it tastes sensational. You can find goat meat at a halal butcher or a Mexican meat market, or, if goat meat isn't available, just use two smaller lamb legs. If you cannot find one or more of the dried chiles called for here, you can substitute other dried chiles.

One 4- to 5-pound bone-in leg of lamb
One 3-pound bone-in leg of goat
2 tablespoons Louis Charles Henley's
   All-Purpose Rub (page 141)

CHILE PURÉE
2 ancho chiles, stemmed and seeded
2 guajillo chiles, stemmed and seeded
2 chipotle chiles, stemmed and seeded

2 tablespoons olive oil
2 celery stalks, chopped
1 onion, chopped
4 garlic cloves, minced
One 14½-ounce can stewed tomatoes
2 carrots, peeled and chopped
Leaves from 3 fresh rosemary
   sprigs, chopped
Leaves from 3 fresh thyme sprigs,
   chopped
Salt and ground black pepper
2 quarts water, plus more as needed
24 small flour tortillas, warmed

Sprinkle the lamb and goat all over with the rub and press the rub into the meat. Wrap the meat in plastic wrap and refrigerate for a few hours to marinate.

Light about 25 charcoal briquettes in a starter chimney and prepare a grill for indirect heat. Place the meat directly over the hot fire and brown, turning often, for 10 to 15 minutes, or until well browned on all sides. Move the meat to the cool side of the grill or to the smoking chamber of an offset barbecue smoker. Put some mesquite wood chips or chunks around the coals and close the lid. Cook the meat at about 250°F, turning it every 30 minutes to ensure that it cooks evenly, for 1½ to 2 hours, or until browned.

Meanwhile, make the chile purée: In a saucepan, combine all the chiles with water to cover, place over low heat, and bring to a simmer. Remove from the heat and let the chiles sit in the hot water for 10 to 20 minutes, or until soft. Drain the chiles, reserving the soaking water, and transfer the chiles to a blender. Process the chiles, adding the soaking water a little at a time as needed, until a smooth purée forms.

In a soup pot, heat the olive oil over medium heat. Add the celery and onion and cook, stirring often, for 5 minutes, or until softened. Add the garlic and cook for a few minutes longer. Add the chile purée and cook for 3 minutes, stirring constantly. Add the tomatoes, carrots, rosemary, thyme, salt and pepper, and water and bring the mixture to a boil. Turn the heat to low and simmer gently while the meat smokes.

When the meat is browned, add more charcoal and wood to the smoker fire. Place a metal roasting pan on the grill directly over the coals, and carefully pour the contents of the soup pot into the pan. Transfer the meat to the roasting pan and simmer and smoke, adding water to the pan if needed to maintain the liquid level, for 1½ hours.

Using fireproof gloves or pot holders, remove the pan from the fire and cover the roast and the roasting pan with aluminum foil, sealing tightly. Return the pan directly over the fire and simmer for 1 to 2 hours, or until the meat is extremely tender. (Or, transfer to a 300°F oven for the same amount of time.) You want the shape of the roast to be intact, but the meat should be very soft.

Remove the meat from the resulting broth and allow to cool slightly. Reserve the broth. Clean the meat away from the bones and chop lightly. Mix the meats in a bowl with some of the chile broth and serve more of the chile broth in a bowl on the side. Or, you can serve some of the broth in small cups as a first course. Accompany the meat with the tortillas and invite guests to make their own tacos.

SERVES 4 TO 6

Barbacoa de Pozo

The earliest barbecue in Texas was the *barbacoa de pozo* of the Tejano ranching culture. In *The Robertsons, the Sutherlands, and the Making of Texas*, author Anne Sutherland observes that the Americans who arrived in Texas in 1820 began to imitate the vaquero culture and style of ranching. "They collected herds of long-horn cattle, which they cooked as barbecue (*barbacoa*) in deep pits as the Mexicans did."

In his book, *Early Tejano Ranching*, Andrés Sáenz describes a wedding celebration held on his family's Tejano ranch in 1937. "They slaughtered a large cow, then barbecued the meat in a hole covered with tin and a fire built over it, to make a pit barbecue, or barbacoa de pozo."

Mexican ranch hands, who were given the offal after the slaughter, made cows' heads the most common form of barbacoa in Texas. But the barbacoa tradition is common on both sides of the border, and the meats cooked in a barbacoa de pozo include sheep and lamb as well as other cuts of beef.

Lengua (Tongue)

BARBACOA IS A HASSLE, BUT LENGUA IS JUST AS good and it's really easy, says Paula Luna of Johnny's Bar-B-Q Pit. Just put the tongue in a slow cooker on Saturday night and you'll have lengua tacos on Sunday morning.

1 beef tongue (about 2 pounds)
Salt and ground black pepper
3 garlic cloves, minced
1 onion, halved

Fresh corn tortillas, lime quarters, chopped onion, fresh cilantro, and Barbecued Tomato Salsa (page 112) or Pico de Gallo (page 113) for serving

The night before you plan to serve, rinse the tongue well, season it with salt and pepper, and put it in a slow cooker with water to cover. Add the garlic and onion to the water. Cook on the high setting for 5 hours, turn the tongue over and add more water if needed to cover, and then turn the heat to low and cook for another 5 hours. The tongue is ready when the skin is hard and the meat is soft.

Transfer the tongue to a cutting board and remove and discard the skin (it should come away easily). Chop the meat finely and put it in a bowl.

Serve immediately with tortillas, lime quarters, chopped onion, cilantro, and salsa.

SERVES 3 OR 4

Bull's-Eye Pork Tenderloin

THIS COLORFUL BARBECUED PORK TENDERLOIN IS RED ON THE OUTSIDE with a bull's-eye of jalapeño chile and crushed garlic in the middle of every slice. If you can't find Mexican achiote paste, bright-red paprika works fine. Serve the sliced tenderloin on toasted buns with sandwich fixin's.

½ cup achiote paste or sweet Hungarian paprika

½ cup orange juice

One 1½-pound pork tenderloin

10 garlic cloves, peeled

4 jalapeño or large serrano chiles

In a bowl, stir together the achiote paste and orange juice to form a smooth paste. Pour into a resealable plastic freezer bag, add the tenderloin, and seal closed. Turn the bag as needed to coat the pork evenly. Put the bag in a container in the refrigerator and marinate overnight.

The next day, smash the garlic cloves with the side of a knife blade until they are flat and shredded. Cut the stem and tip ends off the chiles to form tubes. Slit each chile lengthwise and, without breaking it in half, gently remove the seeds. Gently stuff the hollow chiles with the crushed garlic.

Remove the tenderloin from the marinade and transfer it to a cutting board. Cut off the large ragged end and the small point at the tip to create a uniform cylinder of meat. Reserve the scraps (they make great sausage).

Measure the meat alongside the chiles and cut the cylinder into two pieces that are each two chile lengths. Using a metal skewer, make a lengthwise tunnel in the middle of each pork piece, working from one end to the other. Going slowly, as the meat grain will tend to channel the skewer off to one side, continue working straight through the middle. Widen the hole with your finger. Gently insert the stuffed chiles, end to end, into the tunnel, so that they run the length of each piece of meat. Secure the chiles in place by running a toothpick through the meat and into the chile at each end. (If you don't, the chile will squirt out.)

Set up your smoker for indirect heat with a water pan. Use wood chips, chunks, or logs, and keep up a good level of smoke. Maintain a temperature between 275° and 325°F.

Place the pork in the smoker and cook for 45 minutes to 1 hour, rotating it as needed to expose all sides to the heat. The pork is ready when an instant-read thermometer inserted into the center registers about 145°F for medium.

Allow the roast to rest for 15 minutes. Cut the pork into ¼-inch-thick slices, fan them across a serving platter, and serve.

SERVES 4

Pachanga is a South Texas slang term for an outdoor gathering that includes barbecue, music, and camaraderie. At election time, politicians hold pachangas to win votes.

To turn your backyard barbecue into a proper pachanga, ice the beers in galvanized tubs, string lights in the trees. Set up a horseshoe pit or a bean-bag throwing area and buy a piñata for the kids.

BBQ Pork and Garlicky Guacamole Sandwiches

THE GREAT THING ABOUT COOKING BARBECUE without sauce is that the serving possibilities are limitless. When I barbecue a pork shoulder (Boston butt), I usually serve pulled pork the first night with barbecue sauce and all the trimmings. But when it comes to the leftovers, I make all sorts of things out of them. Here, for instance, is my favorite leftover smoked-pork sandwich. By crisping the leftover pork in a frying pan, you turn the barbecued pork into something that tastes like Mexican *carnitas*.

¼ cup olive oil
1½ pounds Harley's Pork
    Shoulder (page 73),
    chopped
Salt
4 *bolillos* (small sub-type
    sandwich rolls)

1 cup Garlicky Guacamole
    (facing page)
2 teaspoons hot-pepper
    sauce

In a skillet, heat the olive oil over high heat. Season the pork with salt, add to the hot oil, and cook, stirring often, for 5 minutes. Lower the heat a little.

Slit the bolillos lengthwise, cutting just three-fourths of the way through, open them up, and put them on top of the pork to heat. Cook the meat, turning it frequently, for 4 to 6 minutes longer, or until crisp.

Spoon ¼ cup of the guacamole onto each warmed roll. Divide the pork evenly among the rolls and top each portion with ½ teaspoon pepper sauce. Serve immediately.

SERVES 4

Garlicky Guacamole

IF YOU'RE GOING TO USE THIS BATCH OF GUACAMOLE ON BARBECUED PORK sandwiches, make it super-garlicky. You may need to buy your avocados in advance and leave them on the windowsill until they soften a little. Don't bother trying to make guacamole with firm avocados. And don't buy squishy ones—they'll be black inside.

3 ripe avocados, halved, pitted, and peeled
3 serrano chiles, seeded and chopped
1 onion, finely diced
4 garlic cloves, minced, or more to taste

½ cup chopped fresh cilantro
1½ tablespoons fresh lemon juice
Salt

In a bowl, combine the avocados, chiles, onion, garlic, cilantro, and lemon juice and mash with a fork until creamy, then season with salt.

Serve immediately. Guacamole discolors quickly, so it is best not to try to keep it too long.

MAKES ABOUT 2½ CUPS

Adrian Lopez
GONZALES FOOD MARKET

Third-generation pitmaster Adrian Lopez moonlights as a guitarist in a rock 'n' roll band.

Gonzales Food Market Macaroni Salad

SLIGHTLY SWEET MACARONI SALAD WITH raisins is a favorite at the old Gonzales Food Market in Gonzales.

8 ounces elbow macaroni	¼ cup raisins
½ cup chopped onion	1 cup mayonnaise
½ cup chopped celery	Salt and ground
2 carrots, peeled and grated	black pepper

Bring a large saucepan filled with water to a boil. Add the macaroni and cook just until tender, according to package directions. Drain into a colander, rinse with cold water, and drain again, shaking off any excess water.

In a large bowl, combine the cooked macaroni, onion, celery, carrots, raisins, and mayonnaise and mix well. Season with salt and pepper. Cover and refrigerate until well chilled before serving.

SERVES 4

Borracho Beans

BORRACHO MEANS "DRUNK," AND IT REFERS TO THE BEER IN THE COOKING liquid for these popular South Texas beans. If you're cooking beans and pork roast at the same time, you can use the fatty pieces of pork that you remove while carving to add flavor to the beans. Otherwise, use some bacon.

2 cups dried pinto beans

4 cups water

One 12-ounce can beer

1 garlic clove, minced

½ onion, finely chopped

3 fresh epazote sprigs

1 tablespoon guajillo chile powder

½ teaspoon ground cumin

1 cup finely chopped fatty cooked pork scraps or uncooked bacon

One 15-ounce can tomatoes, chopped and with their juice

1 teaspoon salt

Pick over the beans and rinse well. Transfer the beans to a pot and add the water, beer, garlic, onion, epazote, chile powder, cumin, pork, tomatoes with their juices, and salt. Bring to a boil over medium-high heat and cook for 1 hour. Turn the heat to the lowest setting and simmer very gently for 3 to 4 hours, or until the beans are soft, but intact. (Keep the level of the liquid a good inch or so above the beans at all times, adding more water as needed.) Alternatively, cook the beans, liquid, and seasonings in a slow cooker on the high setting for 1 hour, then cook on the low setting for 12 hours.

Taste and adjust the seasoning. Using a slotted spoon, transfer the beans to a serving dish. Pour the broth into a bowl and serve as a side dish to the beans.

SERVES 6 TO 8

Cocinero Juan Cesares prepares barbecue for the cowboys during a roundup on a South Texas ranch.

Pickled Jalapeños

THESE "TEXAS PICKLES" ARE EASY TO MAKE. PUT A FEW BIG JARS UP IN THE fall when chiles flood the supermarkets, and they should last you quite a while.

30 jalapeño chiles

2 carrots, peeled and cut on the diagonal into ½-inch slices

1 small onion, cut through the stem end into 8 wedges

5 cups distilled white vinegar

1 teaspoon pickling salt

In a large heatproof bowl, combine the chiles, carrots, and onion.

Pour the vinegar into a saucepan, add the pickling salt, and bring to a boil over high heat. Remove from the heat, pour over the vegetables, and stir until all of the ingredients are well mixed. Place a plate on top of the vegetables to keep them submerged in the hot liquid. Let cool to room temperature.

Transfer the mixture to two 2-quart nonreactive containers with lids and cap tightly. Refrigerate for 24 hours before serving. They will keep for up to 1 month.

MAKES ABOUT 4 QUARTS

Jalapeño Potato Salad

FETA, JALAPEÑOS, AND BLACK OLIVES MAKE THIS A VERY FLAVORFUL and somewhat elegant potato salad. Serve it on the side with Gerardo's Barbacoa de Borrego (page 222) or any elaborate barbecue spread.

4 large potatoes, peeled and cut into
   ¾-inch cubes
¼ cup Dijon mustard
¼ cup white wine vinegar
2 garlic cloves, crushed
¼ teaspoon salt
¼ teaspoon ground black pepper

½ cup olive oil
One 3½-ounce can pitted black
   olives, drained
¼ cup thinly sliced green onions
6 ounces feta cheese, crumbled
4 jalapeño chiles, seeded and chopped

Place the potatoes in a large saucepan, cover with water, and bring to a boil over high heat. Turn the heat to low and simmer for 10 minutes, or until the potatoes are tender.

While the potatoes are cooking, in a large bowl, whisk together the mustard, vinegar, garlic, salt, and pepper. Slowly whisk in the olive oil until emulsified.

When the potatoes are ready, drain well and add to the dressing in the bowl along with the olives, green onions, feta, and jalapeños. Stir and toss gently to mix well. Serve chilled or at room temperature.

SERVES 6

SMOKING BEEF

Clods, Sirloins,
and Briskets

John Lewis seasons a brisket
at La Barbecue in Austin.

he Texas cattle boom got its start in 1867, when cowboys took their first herds up the Chisholm Trail to the railheads and northern markets. Steers that were rounded up for free in South Texas sold for forty dollars a head at the end of the trail—fortunes were made in a matter of months.

Within a few years, millions of longhorns had been rounded up and taken to market. After the Comanches and the buffalo were killed off, cattlemen took over the vast grasslands of western Texas. Enormous ranches of hundreds of thousands of acres were tended by just a handful of cowboys.

Barbecuing whole steers was already popular at civic barbecues before the Civil War. After the war, thanks to the emerging Texas cattle industry, the market was flooded with beef. In 1873, the best beef cuts were selling for four cents a pound at meat markets in Austin. The forequarter cuts were what people used for barbecue.

The steer's forequarters were typically cut into six- to eight-pound bone-in joints and cooked over hot coals in an open pit, but the lean range-fed beef required continuous basting for up to twenty-four hours. A cotton mop was used, and the basting liquid, generally cooking oil and a little vinegar, was mixed in buckets.

As meat packing became a national industry, cattle raised in Texas were shipped off and fattened on feedlots. Texas meat markets didn't slaughter their own cattle anymore. Boxed beef, which was introduced in the 1960s, was originally just an easier way to ship a whole steer by railcar. Butchers were obliged to buy the whole animal, which came in seven boxes. In the early 1970s, it first became possible to buy boxes of particular cuts of beef. A book titled *The Meat Buyer's Guide* lists the cuts by number. For the first time, barbecue joints weren't obliged to cook the chuck, shoulder, and other forequarter cuts. Instead, they were free to order the cuts of their choice from packing houses.

Some old meat markets began to barbecue shoulder clods; some cowboy barbecue restaurants in West Texas started to feature sirloins. But what most Texas barbecue joints ordered was boneless brisket.

Although the entire brisket actually includes several bones and some hard fat, the cut that Texas barbecue men call brisket is officially known as Item No. 120, "beef brisket, deckle-off, boneless," by the Institutional Meat Purchase Specifications and the North American Meat Processors Association (IMPS and NAMP, respectively). Boneless brisket was well suited to the barbecue business. It was relatively cheap, and the flat provided a uniform slice of meat

to each customer. (Today, barbecued brisket has become so popular that it isn't that cheap anymore.)

Although brisket is widely available, it is a major challenge for the home barbecuer. Like a pot roast, brisket must be cooked for a long time to become tender. There is just no way to hurry up the process. "There is no medium-rare to this part of the steer. It's either totally cooked and edible or it's not," warns Jim Goode of Goode Company Barbecue in Houston.

Even when you follow all of the recipe instructions to the letter, brisket often comes out dry. That's why it is considered the true test of barbecue skill in Texas. It's hard to mess up a pork roast, but it's easy to ruin a brisket. Before you decide to try it, I suggest you think it through carefully.

First, consider your equipment. You couldn't even fit a brisket on a small Weber, and even if you could, think of the hassle of refueling. To maintain a 250°F fire for twelve to fifteen hours, you need to refuel around once an hour. With a barrel or a bigger rig, you're in much better shape. The farther you can get the brisket from the fire, the easier it is to cook.

If you have the equipment, the next question is, are you going to cook an old-fashioned brisket with the fat cap attached, or are you going to trim the fat and try to cook a new-style brisket with a thick, crunchy bark?

The follow-up question is, are you going to be a pragmatist and wrap the brisket in aluminum foil or butcher paper after you get a nice color and smoke level, or are you going to be a purist and smoke it all the way? Wrapping a brisket helps ensure a tender finished product. Many famous barbecue joints wrap theirs, so why shouldn't you?

"Because wrapping a brisket in foil ruins the smoke ring and makes the meat mushy. You will never win a barbecue cook-off with foil-wrapped brisket," says Harley Goerlitz.

If you do wrap it in foil, are you going to keep it on the smoker or finish it in the oven? Some people say there isn't any difference. Most Texans base this decision on how hot it is outside. When the outdoor temperature exceeds 95°F (as it often does in Texas for six months of the year), Texans are loath to turn on the oven. There is something perverse (not to mention expensive) about simultaneously heating and cooling your house. So finishing a foil-wrapped brisket on the smoker isn't always a culinary decision.

There are also some Texans who cook a brisket in the oven from start to finish. Benny Wade Clewis, for instance, grew up eating East Texas–style barbecue and wishes he still could. Last time I heard from Clewis, he was incarcerated in the Darrington men's penitentiary near Rosharon, where he was working in the kitchen. When he gets a chance to make a brisket these days, he makes it in the oven with liquid smoke.

"The kind you make in the oven ain't as good as the real thing," Clewis told me when I sampled his cooking at the prison many years ago. "But it's as close as I'm gonna get." I asked for his recipe and he sent it to me in a letter.

If you love beef but aren't ready for the level of commitment required by brisket, lots of other alternatives exist. Rick Schmidt at Kreuz Market recommends shoulder roasts—a faster cooking and much more forgiving cut of beef. He also smokes prime rib, which may be the easiest and tastiest version of barbecued beef around.

Beef ribs can be even trickier than brisket. I've included a couple of recipes for the square-cut short ribs that are easy to find at the grocery store. To cook the big Fred Flintstone–size plate ribs, just substitute the ribs in your favorite recipe for brisket. The seasoning and timing are just about the same.

The brisket recipes here include complicated and challenging recipes for purists who want to try to win a trophy, "new school" brisket recipes from the young pitmasters and competitors who are wowing food writers, and some easy recipes—including the easiest recipe of all, the Benny Wade Clewis recipe that calls for a brisket cooked with liquid smoke in the oven. Pick your level of difficulty and get after it.

When you can consistently turn out a moist and tender barbecued brisket, you have passed Texas barbecue's PhD exam.

HOW TO SLICE A BRISKET

When your brisket is done, allow it to rest at room temperature for 15 minutes or so before carving. If it's wrapped, you will want to unwrap it before resting. (A wrapped brisket is still cooking, however slowly.)

Brisket starts getting dried out soon after you slice it. Which means that carving a brisket in advance and setting the platter of sliced meat on the table is a terrible idea. Don't even unwrap the brisket until 15 minutes before serving, and don't start carving until everyone is ready to eat.

Old-school barbecue joints cook the brisket with the large fat cap attached. You can remove the fat cap before you slice (Fig. 1). Or you can slice right through and serve each slice with the fat still attached, like Vencil Mares does at Taylor Café. Fat-averse diners can cut the fat away at the table.

If you are cooking a new school brisket, you definitely want to carve straight through the whole brisket and serve each slice with some rendered fat and spicy bark attached.

Brisket has a juicy side (the point) and a lean side (the flat). The idea is to slice as much meat against the grain as possible. Cut the dried-up tip off the end of the flat and look to see exactly which way the grain is running (Fig. 2). Angle your carving knife to slice the flat against the grain.

Carve the flat into slices about a quarter of an inch thick. Slice the point into heftier slices of around a half inch thick. When you get to the point, the grain will be running in two different directions. Cut between the two and separate them. Carve the tapered end of the flat, then spin the meat of the juicy point around 90 degrees and cut across the grain (Fig. 3).

To keep your brisket slices juicy, serve the meat as soon as it's carved. The best idea is to place each slice directly onto someone's plate or on top of a prepared sandwich. Slice more as you need it, not before. Gather the juices and small scraps of meat left behind after you carve the meat and add these to the barbecue sauce if you are serving any.

While the old meat markets in Central Texas offer barbecue sauce begrudgingly, if at all, in other parts of the state, barbecue sauce is very popular with brisket. East Texans tend to cook their briskets extremely well-done and serve the meat swimming in barbecue sauce.

Leftover brisket makes great breakfast tacos. It's most often chopped up, mixed with barbecue sauce, and served on hamburger buns with pickles and onions (see page 259).

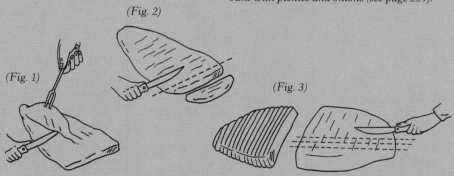

(Fig. 2)

(Fig. 1)

(Fig. 3)

John Fullilove
SMITTY'S

John Fullilove was the pitmaster at Smitty's when the barbecue joint took over from Kreuz Market in 1999. "We are going back to Edgar Schmidt's original recipes," Fullilove promised at the time. "The sausage we make now tastes like the sausage used to taste fifty years ago." In 2012, John Fullilove went to Bee Cave to help open Schmidt Family Barbecue.

Lockhart Prime Rib

THE BARBECUED PRIME RIB AT SMITTY'S AND Kreuz Market is incredibly tender. "I don't know why anybody wants to cook a brisket at home," said John Fullilove. "If I'm cooking at home, I'm going to get a nice cut like a sirloin or a rib roast and smoke it at 300° to 350°F," he says. "I'd just season it with salt and pepper. This kind of barbecued beef roast is perfect for Christmas dinner.

1½ cups Heath Ray's Rub (page 76)

One 3-bone beef rib roast, 3½ to 4 pounds (USDA Prime, Certified Angus [CAB], or other USDA Choice branded beef preferred)

Sprinkle the roast all over with the rub, pressing it into the meat. Let the roast to come to room temperature.

Set up your smoker for indirect heat with a water pan. Use wood chips, chunks, or logs, and keep up a good level of smoke. Maintain a temperature between 325° and 350°F (or as hot as your smoker will allow without charring the meat).

Place the roast in the smoker and cook for 2 hours, rotating it to expose all sides to the heat. Continue cooking, checking and turning every 30 minutes until an instant-read thermometer inserted into the center of the roast away from bone registers about 135°F for medium-rare. This should take 3 to 4 hours total.

Remove the roast from the smoker and let rest for 15 minutes. The temperature should rise to 140°F during resting. Carve the roast away from the bones and then cut the meat against the grain into 1-inch-thick slices and serve.

SERVES 6 TO 8

Maurice Mikeska's Tri-Tip

BRISKET WAS NEVER SERVED AT MAURICE MIKESKA'S LUNCHBOX, HIS TINY restaurant on Merchant Street in El Campo. The only cut of beef on Mikeska's original menu was tri-tip roast. Tri-tip, also known as triangle roast, is an economical cut from the bottom sirloin that includes quite a bit of internal marbling, so it stays moist. It's the favorite cut of California barbecuers.

Thinly sliced, medium-rare tri-tip tastes great with pickles and onions on barbecue sandwiches, Tejano-style on flour tortillas with salsa, or California-style on sourdough garlic bread.

1 USDA Choice beef tri-tip roast (about
   2½ pounds; Black Angus or other
   branded beef preferred)

6 tablespoons Louis Charles Henley's
   All-Purpose Rub (page 141)
3 slices bacon

Let the roast come to room temperature. Sprinkle the roast all over with the rub, pressing it into the meat. Lay the bacon slices over the top of the roast.

Set up your smoker for indirect heat with a water pan. Use wood chips, chunks, or logs, and keep up a good level of smoke. Maintain a temperature between 275° and 300°F.

Place the roast in the smoker and cook for 15 minutes, then begin rotating it to expose all sides to the heat. Reposition the bacon as necessary to keep it on top of the roast. Continue cooking, checking and turning every 15 minutes, until an instant-read thermometer inserted into the center of the roast registers about 135°F for medium-rare. This should take 45 to 60 minutes total.

Remove the roast from the smoker and let rest for 15 minutes. The temperature should rise to 140°F during resting. (The USDA recommends 140°F.) Cut the meat against the grain into extremely thin slices (a deli slicer works great for this). Serve on a mixed meat plate or on sandwiches.

SERVES 6

Rick Schmidt's Shoulder Roast

AT KREUZ MARKET IN LOCKHART, SHOULDER CLOD IS ONE OF THE MOST popular beef cuts. "It's a nice cut of beef, so you can serve it a little pink," says pitmaster Rick Schmidt. But a whole untrimmed shoulder clod weighs around twenty pounds— a little large for the average home smoker. And the carving is really tricky, as the grain goes three different ways. "A shoulder roast is the same cut of meat, and it's an easier size for home barbecuing," Schmidt advises. The only problem is that without all the fat, the meat tends to dry out. That's why I've added the bacon.

1 USDA Choice boneless beef shoulder roast (about 3 pounds; USDA Prime, CAB, or other branded beef preferred)

2 teaspoons salt

1 teaspoon finely ground black pepper

1 teaspoon cracked black pepper

¼ teaspoon cayenne pepper

3 slices bacon

Let the roast come to room temperature. In a small bowl, stir together the salt, both black peppers, and cayenne. Sprinkle the roast all over with the seasoning mixture, pressing it into the meat. Lay the bacon slices over the top of the roast.

Set up your smoker for indirect heat with a water pan. Use wood chips, chunks, or logs, and keep up a good level of smoke. Maintain a temperature between 300° and 350°F (or as hot as your smoker will allow without charring the meat).

Place the roast in the smoker and cook for 2 hours, rotating to expose all sides to the heat. Reposition the bacon as necessary to keep it on top of the roast. Continue cooking, checking and turning every 15 minutes, until an instant-read thermometer inserted into the center of the roast registers about 140°F for medium. This should take about 2 hours total.

Remove the roast from the smoker and let rest for 15 minutes. The temperature should rise to 145°F during resting. Cut the meat against the grain into thin slices and serve.

SERVES 6 TO 8

BEEF RIBS

Louie Mueller Barbecue in Taylor is justly famous for its beef ribs, which are featured on its menu daily. Gonzales Food Market used to serve crispy smoked square-cut short ribs, but discontinued them. Others have tried cooking ribs, but without consistent success. Beef ribs used to be the worst bet on the barbecue menu. Now, they've moved into the spotlight.

Justin Fourton at Pecan Lodge serves the most-talked-about beef ribs in Texas. They average a pound and a half each and sell for more than twenty-five dollars apiece. "Before, the barbecued beef ribs were always dry and chewy," says Ronnie Killen, who cooks USDA Prime beef ribs at Killen's Barbecue in Pearland. "Now, cooked right, they are like the fatty end of the brisket but without all the fat."

A well-cooked USDA Prime or Choice beef rib can be just as succulent as a perfectly cooked brisket but with a softer, silkier texture. In Korean barbecue, sliced and marinated short ribs (known as kalbi or galbi) are rated alongside rib-eye (bulgogi) as the best cuts of beef. Top chefs raised the profile of braised beef ribs, and that popularity spilled over into the realm of barbecue.

The two big problems professional and amateur pitmasters have with beef ribs are the serving size and the confusing nomenclature. The term beef ribs is used to describe cuts from several different parts of the animal. Texas pitmasters often refer to the item numbers from the IMPS/NAMP Meat Buyers' Guide to specify which ribs they are talking about.

The smaller ones are called chuck short ribs (No. 130 in The Meat Buyer's Guide), and they are easily carved into just the right size for a single serving. These are the square-cut ribs found in the supermarket meat case. The giant ones are called plate short ribs (No. 123A in The Meat Buyer's Guide).

Pitmaster Wayne Mueller clowns around with a rack of beef ribs at Louie Mueller Barbecue in Taylor.
Photo by Robert Lerma

Ray Lopez
GONZALES FOOD MARKET

Ray Lopez is a pitmaster at the Gonzales Food Market, which was opened by the Lopez family near the square in Gonzales in 1959. It started as a food store but soon became well known for its coarse-ground sausage and smoked meats, especially the beef ribs.

Ray Lopez's Beef Ribs

RAY LOPEZ USED TO MAKE THESE BEEF RIBS at Gonzales Food Market on special occasions. The key to this recipe is to put the ribs in a pan in the smoker and then to turn them in the melted fat as they cook to crisp them up. It's like frying and smoking them at the same time.

2 to 3 pounds beef short ribs (square cut)

3 tablespoons Heath Ray's Rub (page 76)

Set up your smoker for indirect heat. Use wood chips, chunks, or logs, and keep up a good level of smoke. Maintain a temperature between 275° and 325°F.

Sprinkle the ribs all over with the rub, pressing it into the meat. Place the ribs in a roasting pan and put the pan in the smoker close to the heat source. Smoke for about 3 hours, turning the ribs often to crisp them on all sides. The ribs are done when they are falling apart.

Remove the ribs from the smoker and serve hot.

SERVES 4

Smoke-Braised Beef Ribs

THIS RECIPE STARTS OUT LIKE RAY LOPEZ'S BEEF RIBS ON PAGE 246, BUT here a braising liquid is added to the pan. The ribs come out with a smoky flavor and a meltingly soft braised texture. Let them get well-done before you add the hot braising liquid.

6 beef short ribs (square cut)
2 tablespoons Heath Ray's Rub
   (page 76)
1 tablespoon vegetable oil
½ onion, chopped

3 garlic cloves, chopped
One 12-ounce bottle cane
   sugar–sweetened Dr Pepper
2 ancho chiles
1 cup molasses

Set up your smoker for indirect heat with a water pan.

Sprinkle the ribs all over with the rub, pressing it into the meat. Place the ribs in a roasting pan and put the pan in the smoker over medium-hot coals. Add some wood chunks or chips to the coals. When the ribs start to sizzle, turn them. Continue to cook the ribs in the pan for 1 hour, turning them as needed to caramelize on all sides. Move the pan to the cool side of the grill if the meat begins to burn or stick.

In a skillet, heat the vegetable oil over medium heat on the stove top. Add the onion and cook, stirring often, for about 5 minutes, until softened. Add the garlic and cook for 1 minute longer. Add the Dr Pepper and bring to a boil, then lower the heat to a simmer and add the chiles. When the chiles have softened, about 10 minutes, remove them with a little of the liquid and purée in a blender. Return the purée to the skillet.

Add more wood and charcoal to the fire if needed. When the ribs are well browned, pour an equal amount of the molasses over each rib and turn each rib to coat evenly. Add the hot Dr Pepper mixture to the roasting pan, then place the pan directly over the hot coals so the liquid comes to a simmer.

Cover the grill and allow the ribs to smoke and simmer for 1 hour, turning the ribs often. Cover the pan with aluminum foil and let the ribs steam for 30 minutes.

Remove the pan from the grill and transfer the ribs to a serving dish. Stir the braising liquid and molasses in the pan together and pour over the ribs. Serve immediately.

SERVES 2 TO 4

Jim Goode's "Plugged" Brisket

THIS RECIPE EMPLOYS A VARIATION ON AN OLD TECHNIQUE CALLED *LARDING*. Larding involves inserting pieces of fat into the lean part of a roast in order to improve the tenderness. This used to be done with a tool called a larding needle. Jim Goode, founder of Houston's Goode Company Barbecue, does the same thing with plugs of fat cut from the underside of the brisket. He seasons them and inserts them into slits cut into the lean meat.

Besides running one of the top barbecue pits in Texas, Jim Goode is also a former chuck-wagon cook-off competitor and an all-around expert on Texas cookery.

Packer's cut (untrimmed) USDA Select beef brisket (8 to 10 pounds)
3 garlic cloves, cut into 24 thin slivers
1 cup Jim Goode's Beef Rub (facing page)
1 tablespoon olive oil
6 cups Jim Goode's Barbecue Mop (page 250)

On the lean side of the brisket, you'll find some pieces of hard fat. Remove some of the fat with a knife, cut it into ¼-inch-thick slices, and then cut the slices into twelve square plugs about 1 inch long.

In a bowl, combine the plugs and garlic slivers with 2 tablespoons of the rub and the olive oil, and turn with a spatula to mix well.

Using a paring knife, make twelve 1-inch-deep slits on the lean side of the brisket at regular intervals. Widen each hole with your finger and force a fat plug and two garlic slivers into each slit. Force them in deeply or they will pop out. Repeat to use up all the plugs and slivers. Season the brisket all over with the remaining rub, pressing it into the meat. Wrap the brisket in plastic wrap or place in a resealable plastic freezer bag and refrigerate overnight.

Set up your smoker for indirect heat with a water pan. Use wood chips, chunks, or logs, and keep up a good level of smoke. Maintain a temperature between 225° and 275°F.

Place the brisket, fat-side up, in the smoker as far away from the fire as possible. Cook, mopping the brisket with the mop sauce every 30 minutes and rotating so it cooks evenly, keeping the fat side up at all times. Add charcoal and/or wood every hour or so to keep the fire burning evenly. The meat is done when an instant-read thermometer inserted into the thick end registers 185°F, or when a probe goes through with little resistance. This should take 12 to 15 hours.

Remove the brisket from the smoker and let rest for 15 minutes.

(See "How to Slice a Brisket" on page 241 for serving tips.)

SERVES 10 TO 12

Jim Goode's Beef Rub

SERIOUS BARBECUERS HAVE THEIR OWN RUB recipe. Jim Goode was nice enough to share his, but you'll want to concoct your own.

¼ cup salt, or to taste

2½ tablespoons firmly packed dark brown sugar

2 tablespoons paprika

2 teaspoons dry mustard

2 teaspoons garlic powder

2 teaspoons onion powder

1½ teaspoons dried basil

1 teaspoon ground bay leaf

¾ teaspoon ground coriander

¾ teaspoon ground savory

¾ teaspoon dried thyme

¾ teaspoon ground black pepper

¾ teaspoon ground white pepper

⅛ teaspoon ground cumin

Combine all of the ingredients in a bowl and mix well, then transfer to a shaker jar. The rub will keep at room temperature for up to 3 months.

MAKES 1 CUP

Jim Goode's Brisket Tips

Timing: The rule of thumb for timing a brisket is 1 hour per 1 pound at 250°F, but you must add another 15 minutes for every time you open the lid or let the fire go below that temperature. Most cooks figure 1½ hours per 1 pound to be safe, or 15 hours for a 10-pound brisket.

Yield: Once you remove the fat cap and allow for shrinkage, a brisket yields about half of the weight you started with, so a 10-pound brisket should yield around 5 pounds of cooked meat.

Jim Goode's Barbecue Mop

THIS MOP IS SO GOOD THAT YOU'LL BE TEMPTED TO EAT IT LIKE SOUP. The combination of butter and bacon makes one of the most flavorful moisturizing marinades you'll ever taste.

4 cups beef stock

2 bay leaves

1 teaspoon dried oregano

2 tablespoons butter

¼ cup chopped onion

¼ cup chopped celery

¼ cup chopped green bell pepper

¼ cup minced garlic

2 tablespoons Jim Goode's Beef Rub (page 249)

½ teaspoon dry mustard

½ teaspoon salt

½ teaspoon ground black pepper

½ teaspoon ground white pepper

¼ teaspoon cayenne pepper

Grated zest and juice of 2 lemons

2 tablespoons soy sauce

2 tablespoons white wine vinegar

1 tablespoon olive oil

1 tablespoon Asian sesame oil

1 pound thinly sliced bacon, finely chopped

In a saucepan, bring the stock to a boil over high heat. Add the bay leaves and oregano and turn the heat to a gentle simmer.

In a skillet, melt the butter over medium-high heat. Add the onion, celery, bell pepper, garlic, beef rub, mustard, salt, black pepper, white pepper, and cayenne. Cook, stirring often, for 5 to 7 minutes, or until the onion wilts. Add the warmed stock, lemon zest, lemon juice, soy sauce, vinegar, olive oil, and sesame oil and stir to mix.

In a separate skillet, cook the bacon over medium heat, stirring often, for 3 to 5 minutes, or until the fat has rendered and the bacon is soft. Add the bacon and drippings to the stock mixture and simmer for about 1 hour, or until reduced by one-fourth.

Remove from the heat, let cool, and use immediately, or transfer to an airtight container and store in the refrigerator for up to 2 weeks.

MAKES 6 CUPS

Beef comes first, but Texas barbecue is equally famous for its variety.

Edgar Black Jr. on Brisket

"When I was a kid, a cattleman came over to our house one day. It was during the Depression. We lived out in the country then. My dad was out of work at the time and this cattleman wasn't selling any cattle. So he told my dad that if we would move to Lockhart and run the empty grocery store there, then this guy would give him some cattle. So we moved to Lockhart and took over the store.

"In those days, round steaks, porterhouse, and sirloin were all anybody would buy. Nobody ate ground meat, so you always had the fore-quarters left over. Nowadays you make chuck roasts and such out of it, but back then you barbecued it. Bone-in forequarter cuts were the most common barbecue meat in Texas. All the meat markets and grocery stores sold it. I was still buying cattle at auction and butchering them myself until the 1950s. But

Edgar Black Jr.'s Overnight Brisket

EDGAR BLACK JR. DOESN'T USE A RUB AND HE doesn't use a mop at Black's Barbecue in Lockhart. "The only seasoning is post oak," he says. He starts a big fire in the old brick smoker at 8:00 P.M. and lets it burn down through the night while the brisket cooks. In the morning, he starts the fire back up and cooks the brisket another three hours.

Packer's cut (untrimmed) USDA Select beef brisket (8 to 10 pounds)

Salt and ground black pepper

Season the brisket all over with salt and pepper and let it come to room temperature.

Set up your smoker for indirect heat with a water pan. Use wood chips, chunks, or logs, and keep up a good level of smoke. Maintain a temperature of around 300°F.

Place the brisket, fat-side up, in the smoker as far away from the fire as possible. Tend the fire to maintain a temperature of around 300°F for 2 to 3 hours. Then add a good amount of fuel, close the flues down to keep the fire at a slow smolder, and go to bed.

In the morning, restart the fire. Remove the brisket from the barbecue so that it doesn't get covered with ashes when you add the coals. When the fire is going, add wood and begin smoking again for another 2 to 3 hours. The meat is done when an instant-read thermometer inserted into the thick end registers 185°F, or when a probe goes through with little resistance.

Remove the brisket from the smoker and let rest for 15 minutes. (See "How to Slice a Brisket" on page 241 for serving tips.)

SERVES 10 TO 12

Cooper's Cowboy Brisket

AT COOPER'S IN LLANO, MESQUITE IS BURNED down to coals in a separate fireplace and then the hot coals are shoveled into a pit. Grills are placed about eighteen inches above the coals, and briskets are cooked over the coals for four hours. They are then wrapped in aluminum foil and held for a few more hours.

The best way to imitate this technique is to grill a brisket over mesquite coals in a barrel-type smoker or a Weber for as long as you can manage to keep it from burning. Then wrap it in foil and finish it over indirect heat or in the oven.

Packer's cut (untrimmed) USDA Select beef brisket (8 to 10 pounds)	Salt and ground black pepper

Season the brisket all over with salt and pepper and let it come to room temperature.

Light mesquite chunks in a starter chimney. Burn the wood down to coals and pour the hot coals into your firebox. Light another batch of mesquite chunks a few minutes later.

Place the brisket on the grill fat-side up, directly over the coals. Cooking the brisket over the coals for 3 to 4 hours is optimal, but just try to grill it for as long as you can without burning it. Then wrap the brisket in heavy-duty aluminum foil and continue cooking on the grill or in a roasting pan in a 250°F oven. The meat is done when an instant-read thermometer inserted into the thick end registers 185°F, or when a probe goes through with little resistance. This should take another 3 to 4 hours, though the timing will vary depending on how long you grill the brisket before wrapping it. Remove the brisket from the smoker and let rest for 15 minutes. (See "How to Slice a Brisket" on page 241 for serving tips.)

SERVES 10 TO 12

when they started sending cattle up north to be fattened in feedlots, the slaughtering business moved north, too.

"And then you ordered your meat from a packing house instead of cutting it up yourself. So there wasn't any reason to barbecue forequarters anymore. I was the first one around here to start ordering brisket. In the 1950s, we raised our price. People thought it was pretty outrageous. We started charging a dollar a pound for barbecue."

THE NEW SCHOOL OF BRISKET

The new-school Texas brisket is made with premium-grade meat, so it is melt-in-your-mouth tender. It's fattier than the brisket Texans are used to eating, but the fat on the higher-grade meat renders to a buttery perfection. The rendered fat is topped with a spicy crust (called a bark) that's created by rubbing spices into the fat cap before the brisket is cooked (see Robert Sierra's Brisket on page 256).

This new-school brisket has several variations in cooking style. Some barbecue-joint pitmasters sprinkle the seasoning directly on the fat cap without wetting it. Some wet the brisket with pickle juice or slather it with mustard first. And still others use brown mustard instead of the yellow stuff.

At Franklin Barbecue in Austin, Aaron Franklin seasons lightly trimmed Creekstone Farms Natural USDA Prime briskets with nothing but salt and pepper, smokes them for six to eight hours, and wraps them in butcher paper at around 180°F. His crew was spritzing the briskets with diluted Worcestershire sauce just before wrapping them the day I watched them cook, but Franklin says they don't do that anymore. The briskets are ready when they reach 200° to 203°F.

At Killen's in Pearland, untrimmed Creekstone Farms USDA Prime brisket is cooked with salt and pepper as well, but the rub includes three different grinds of black pepper (fine, medium, and half-cracked).

Justin Fourton at Pecan Lodge in Dallas doesn't think the difference in quality between Certified Angus Beef (CAB) briskets and USDA Prime briskets is worth the steep difference in price. He trims some excess fat from CAB briskets, but recommends leaving about ¼ inch of fat on top. Then he seasons the briskets with his secret spice mix (I'm guessing garlic powder and paprika along with the salt and pepper) and cooks them for fourteen to eighteen hours, until they reach 190°F. Fourton likes his meat springy, not falling apart.

Justin Fourton, pitmaster at Pecan Lodge in Dallas, recommends CAB briskets.

Learning where a brisket comes from at BBQ Summer Camp

COMPARING BRISKET GRADES

At BBQ Summer Camp and Camp Brisket, we have conducted multiple blind taste tests to compare five grades of brisket. Graduate students in the Texas A&M Meat Science program cook all five briskets on the same smoker with an identical seasoning of salt and pepper. Here are some notes on the rankings:

USDA Prime: *Tender, juicy, and flavorful. This is the most consistent winner in the blind taste tests and your best bet for cooking New School brisket.*

Where to get it: Ask the butcher at your neighborhood supermarket to order you a packer's cut (untrimmed) USDA Prime brisket. It may be a few days before it arrives. If the butcher is no help, you can call a restaurant purveyor and order one for pickup at the warehouse. Be prepared to pay cash.

The Master Chef Prime Whole Brisket from Kansas-based meat supplier Creekstone Farms is popular among cook-off competitors and upscale barbecue joints. Expect to pay $100 to $150 plus shipping for one USDA Prime brisket. You can order them online at www.creekstonefarms.com.

Certified Angus Beef (CAB): *A little denser than Prime, with a wonderful flavor and moist texture. Ranked second or third in taste tests.*

Where to get it: CAB is the most popular branded beef among restaurants. CAB comes from the top two-thirds of USDA Choice. In upscale supermarkets, you can often find Sterling Silver, another leading brand from the top two tiers of USDA Choice. There are lots of other brands, but beware, as not all branded beef is of equal quality. Some of it is just USDA Select from a particular breed of cattle.

USDA Choice: *Ranked a little lower than Prime or CAB, but still a good bet. The second highest USDA grade is made up of three tiers. The top tier is close to USDA Prime and the bottom is close to USDA Select. When you buy steaks, you can look at the marbling and make an educated guess. When you buy brisket, it's a crapshoot.*

Where to get it: Look for USDA Choice brisket at restaurant supply stores and wholesale clubs like Sam's or Costco.

Wagyu: *The most expensive beef on the market scores erratically in blind taste tests. It is so marbled with fat that it tends to fall apart before it reaches the target temperature.*

Where to get it: Wagyu briskets can be ordered online.

USDA Select: *Sometimes a USDA Select brisket will score surprisingly well in a blind taste test, but it's usually the lowest ranked grade. This is the brisket served at your average Texas barbecue joint.*

Where to get it: USDA Select brisket is widely available in grocery stores that sell barbecue cuts.

Robert Sierra's Brisket

NOBODY KNOWS BRISKET BETTER THAN COOK-OFF CHAMPION ROBERT SIERRA, who has won the brisket category in competitions all over the state. But this is not his secret competition recipe. It is his more casual home recipe for friends and family, so customize it as you see fit.

If you like, you can skip the marinade injection step. Pitmasters at busy barbecue joints don't have time for marinades, but cook-off competitors swear by them. The brisket should be cooked from a minimum of 185°F to a maximum of 205°F and sliced without removing the fat. It's served bark, fat, and all—and the best slices come from the fatty end.

Packer's cut (untrimmed) USDA Prime
    beef brisket (10 to 15 pounds)

MARINADE
½ cup flat Coca-Cola
1 cup beef stock
½ teaspoon kosher salt
3 garlic cloves, smashed
10 black peppercorns

¼ cup Worcestershire sauce
¼ cup water
1 cup yellow prepared mustard,
    or more as needed
Garlic powder for sprinkling
Sweet paprika for sprinkling
Chili powder for sprinkling
Cayenne pepper for sprinkling (optional)
Kosher salt
Finely ground black pepper
Coarsely ground black pepper

26 hours before serving

Trim the brisket of any large pieces of hard fat. If necessary, trim the thickest part of the fat cap to an even ¼-inch-thick layer. Put the brisket in a roasting pan.

To make the marinade: In a small saucepan, combine the flat soda, beef stock, salt, garlic, and peppercorns and bring to a boil over high heat. Turn the heat to medium and simmer for 20 minutes, or until the garlic and peppercorns have infused the liquid. Check the seasonings; the liquid should be quite salty. Remove from the heat and let cool. Strain the marinade through a fine strainer to remove all particles.

Inject the marinade into the brisket in eight or ten places, allowing the overflow to gather in the bottom of the pan.

In a spray bottle, combine the Worcestershire, water, and well-strained marinade left over after you have injected the brisket. Set the spray bottle aside.

Spread the mustard over the fat cap of the brisket. Sprinkle the mustard layer first with garlic powder, then with paprika, followed by chili powder, cayenne (if using), salt, and both black peppers, until the mustard is completely covered. Press the spices into the mustard with your palm. If the mustard is still sticky, add more spices. Place the roasting pan with the seasoned brisket in the refrigerator overnight to allow the rub to set.

14 hours before serving

Remove the brisket from the refrigerator and allow it to come to room temperature. Set up your smoker for indirect heat with a water pan. Use wood chips, chunks, or logs, and keep up a good level of smoke. Maintain a temperature of 225° to 275°F.

13 hours before serving

Remove the brisket from the roasting pan; put the brisket, fat-side up, in the smoker; and close the lid. Cook, adding a little fuel every 1 to 1½ hours to maintain a temperature of around 250°F, and mist with the Worcestershire spray at each refueling. Wearing fireproof gloves, gently turn the brisket fat-side down after 6 hours, being careful not to knock off the bark. Spritz the bottom of the brisket with the Worcestershire spray until it is shiny. Season the underside of the brisket with the same sequence of spices but without the mustard. After another 2 hours, test the brisket with an instant-read thermometer. If the internal temperature registers 160°F or higher, it is time to wrap it.

4 to 5 hours before serving

Clean the roasting pan. Wrap the brisket in untreated butcher paper or aluminum foil and place in the clean roasting pan on the barbecue smoker at 250°F or in a 250°F oven.

1 to 2 hours before serving

Timing is the trickiest part. Leave yourself a little wiggle room in case the brisket takes longer than expected. If it is done early and your gang isn't ready to eat yet, lower the temperature and continue to hold the brisket on the barbecue or in the oven—it will be fine for up to 4 hours.

The target temperature is somewhere between 185° and 205°F. Below 185°F, the meat will still be quite firm. It will slice beautifully at 190°F. But most cook-off competitors consider the sweet spot for tenderness to be 200°F. If you let it get much past 205°F, the meat will begin to fall apart when you slice it.

20 minutes before serving

Unwrap the brisket and place it on a cutting board. Allow the brisket to rest for 15 minutes. (See "How to Slice a Brisket" on page 241 for serving tips.)

SERVES 12 TO 15

Darrington Penitentiary Barbecued Brisket

THIS ISN'T THE WAY BENNY WADE CLEWIS REALLY LIKES HIS BRISKET, BUT at Darrington penitentiary he doesn't have any choice in the matter. This recipe might prove handy should you find yourself confined to prison—or a New York apartment. You can use any mop sauce for the cooking liquid.

4 cups beef stock

½ cup cider vinegar

¼ cup liquid smoke

2 bay leaves

2 cups chopped onion

2 cups chopped carrot

½ cup chopped celery

½ cup chopped green bell pepper

¼ cup salt

3 tablespoons minced garlic

¼ cup Worcestershire sauce

1 teaspoon ground black pepper

Packer's cut (untrimmed) USDA Select
    beef brisket (8 to 10 pounds)

In a Dutch oven, combine the beef stock, vinegar, liquid smoke, bay leaves, onion, carrot, celery, bell pepper, salt, garlic, Worcestershire, and black pepper and stir to mix well. Add the brisket and water to cover. Allow to marinate in the refrigerator overnight.

The next day, put the Dutch oven on the stove top over medium heat and bring the contents to a boil, turning the brisket so it doesn't burn. Turn the heat to low and simmer the brisket in the marinade for 1 hour.

Preheat the oven to 350°F.

Transfer the brisket to a cutting board and cut into slices. Put the slices in the Dutch oven with the marinade and transfer the pot to the oven. Cook for 2 hours, or until very tender. Serve hot with a little of the marinade drizzled over the top.

SERVES 10

Robb's Brisket Disaster Sandwiches

I WANTED TO HAVE A BARBECUE ONE SUNDAY, SO I PUT A BRISKET ON THE smoker at 8:00 P.M. on Saturday night and tended the fire carefully until I went to bed at around 11:00 P.M. I intended to get up and check the fire throughout the night, but I didn't wake up until 4:00 A.M. By then, the fire had gone out. The brisket had plenty of smoke flavor, and since I was using a recipe that called for wrapping the brisket in aluminum foil with some mop sauce, I figured I'd just put the wrapped brisket in the oven at 225°F instead of trying to start another fire in the middle of the night.

At 5:00 A.M., I was awakened by the smoke alarm. That's how I learned that you can't put a foil-wrapped brisket directly on the oven rack. It punctures the foil and allows the fat to run all over the oven and smoke up the house.

After I cleaned up the oven, I put the foil-wrapped brisket into a roasting pan and put it back in the oven at around 6:00 A.M., and I went back to sleep. Everything would have worked out fine if I hadn't left the oven on all day. By the time of the barbecue on Sunday night, the brisket was as mushy as pot roast. It still tasted good, however.

What do you do with eight pounds of squishy, overcooked brisket? You chop up the meat, add a little sauce, and make it into the classic Texas barbecue-joint leftover delicacy, chopped beef sandwiches.

Brisket scraps or leftovers

Barbecue sauce of your choice, heated

Hamburger buns or kaiser rolls,
   split and toasted

Onion slices

Pickle slices

Chop the brisket well, removing any fat, and transfer to a bowl. Add enough barbecue sauce to create a sloppy-joe consistency.

Place the bottom halves of the buns, cut-side up, on individual plates. Spoon a generous helping of the chopped brisket mixture onto each bun bottom. Top with the onion and pickle slices, close the sandwiches with the bun tops, and serve.

SERVES 1

ON THE
BARBECUE
TRAIL

Following the Smoke

hree men sit on the bench in front of Dozier's Grocery on FM 359 in rural Fulshear. I pause on the wood-plank front porch for a minute to read the handwritten notes on the bulletin board. A pickup truck honks as it passes by. The three men look up and wave. Inside, the grocery has a small collection of convenience-store items up front and a huge meat market in the back. This is the way Texas barbecue used to be.

As small-town retail districts fade away, some of the oldest barbecue joints in Texas have closed their doors or moved to greener pastures. Meanwhile, in urban Texas strip malls, new barbecue restaurants are decorated to look like old country stores. The high school kids who work there probably don't even know why.

In these new automated operations, employees load meat onto the racks of gas-fired rotisserie ovens, push a button, and go home. The virtual barbecue oven does the rest. The quality of the smoked meat pales in comparison to the taste of meat cooked the old-fashioned way, with nothing but smoke.

These high-tech barbecue ovens do fill a need, however. They make barbecue convenient and consistent. They also solve the building-code and air-pollution problems that make old-fashioned barbecue pits difficult to build in big cities . . . and they are slowly but surely replacing the real thing.

Writer Marshall McLuhan observed, "Because we are benumbed by any new technology—we tend to make the old environment more visible; we do so by turning it into an art form and by attaching ourselves to the objects and atmosphere that characterized it."

Old-fashioned Texas barbecue has become an art form. As each old barbecue joint disappears, the ones that remain become more treasured. Here are some barbecue joints that are worth a visit. Most of them are old places. A few are new places that are reviving the old-fashioned ways. When you're driving around, don't forget to keep your eyes open. You never know when you might happen upon a shade-tree barbecue stand or a little shack that nobody's ever heard of—with the best smoked meat in creation.

The Business of Barbecue

Whenever I see an unlicensed shade-tree barbecue stand along the side of a Texas farm-to-market road, I think of history's first barbecue salesmen—those famous outlaws, the buccaneers.

In the French West Indies, the word for a barbecue grill is *boucan* (from Tupi, a Brazilian language). *Boucanée* means "smoked meat." Hence, the word *buccaneer* is derived from the French word for barbecuer. The buccaneers were a ragtag crew consisting mainly of French and English outlaws and escaped slaves. They hid from the Spanish on the island of Tortuga off the northern coast of Hispaniola in the mid-1600s. Although they would later be known for their seafaring exploits, their original business was smoke-cured meat.

The buccaneers hunted the wild cows and pigs left behind by failed Spanish settlements on Hispaniola. They smoke-cured the meat and sold it to passing ships. But because the Spanish were hunting the buccaneers, the latter banded together for their own protection. Eventually they gave up on the meat business and went to sea. Soon they discovered that capturing Spanish vessels by surprise attack was a lot more lucrative than chasing wild pigs. Before long, the buccaneers came to be known more as fearless seamen than as barbecue purveyors. But many would argue that it was in their first occupation that they made their most significant contribution to humanity.

Like the buccaneers, the owners of Texas barbecue joints are forever at odds with the authorities. Barbecue is, by definition, a primitive cooking process. The health laws in many Texas counties do not allow restaurants to cook outdoors. Folks who have barbecue joints often build tin roofs, screened porches, and other elaborate facades to bring the outdoor cooking indoors (at least technically). In outlaw tradition, the best barbecue generally comes from the joint that is in the most trouble with the health department.

The Barbecue Belt

THE TOWNS OF LOCKHART, TAYLOR, AND ELGIN ARE MAJOR STOPS ON ANY tour of the Central Texas barbecue belt. All three towns are located on rail lines in cotton-farming country. The shopping districts of these towns are nearly empty today; buildings stand unoccupied, and pedestrians are rare, but in their heyday, these were bustling cotton-shipping centers. On a Saturday night during the harvest season fifty years ago, their streets were packed with merchants, farmers, and cotton pickers out for a night on the town.

Lockhart

During the spring 1999 session of the Texas Legislature, the House of Representatives approved a resolution naming Lockhart the Barbecue Capital of Texas. Lockhart barbecue joints draw customers from hundreds of miles around. The style is widely imitated and Lockhart-style barbecue joints with some family connection to the originals can now be found in Dallas (Lockhart Smokehouse), Austin (Schmidt Family Barbecue), and Manhattan (Hill Country Barbecue). While they may serve the same sausage, none of the satellite locations can match the charm of Lockhart.

Black's Barbecue

215 N MAIN STREET

512-398-2712

Established by Edgar Black Sr. in 1932, during the Great Depression, this landmark's first barbecue pits were located in a tin shed behind the combination meat market and grocery store across from the current restaurant location. You can eat "1932 style" on butcher paper, or you can work your way through a cafeteria-style serving line that includes various salads and side dishes.

Chisholm Trail Bar-B-Q

1323 S COLORADO STREET

512-398-6027

In 1978, Floyd Wilhelm sold his fishing boat to raise the money to open this place. "Sometimes, I look back and think I must have been crazy," he says. "Starting a barbecue place here was like opening a ballpark across the street from Yankee Stadium." Nevertheless, Chisholm Trail draws a crowd of regulars every day at lunchtime.

Kreuz Market (pronounced "Krites")

619 N COLORADO STREET

512-398-2361

For many years, Kreuz was called the best barbecue joint in the state by magazines, newspapers, and barbecue writers. The smoked meats are still the finest you may ever taste, but since its move in 1999 to a new location, it has lost some of the tradition that made the experience so impressive. The new location is not a meat market, but it continues in the meat-market tradition. The beef, sausage, and pork are served on brown butcher paper without barbecue sauce. In a bow to modern times, however, pork ribs and several side dishes are now offered.

Smitty's Market

208 S COMMERCE STREET

512-398-9344

This is the original location of Kreuz Market, and the smokers here are more than a hundred years old. Stop by early for some of the best sausage rings in the state. The pork loin is also excellent. Take a tour of the old dining halls, where the knives are still chained to the tables. In the days of the cotton pickers, this not only prevented the disappearance of the knives but also cut down on knife fights.

In 1999, Kreuz Market moved from the downtown location (now Smitty's Market) to this impressive new location down the road.

Taylor

As the home of one of the state's most pleasant competitions, the Taylor International Barbecue Cook-Off, Taylor is a barbecue capital in its own right. Two of the state's most historic barbecue joints lie within a couple of blocks of each other in the city's downtown shopping district. The old center of Taylor has been used as a film set and looks like a time capsule from the 1950s.

Louie Mueller Barbecue

206 W 2ND STREET
512-352-6206

Louie Mueller Barbeque was established in the mid-1940s in a small tin shed in the alley behind Louie Mueller's Complete Food Store. A few years later, Louie opened his second location in south Taylor to accommodate the cotton pickers and farmers who came to town looking for something to eat when they got off work. He moved to the present location in 1959.

Mueller's is consistently rated one of the top barbecue restaurants in the state. The brisket is excellent, and so are the pork ribs. If you want to try the famous beef ribs, come early. Louie Mueller's has side dishes and sauces, as well.

Taylor Cafe

101 N MAIN STREET
512-352-2828

The Taylor Cafe is a tiny beer joint with two bars—a leftover from the days of segregation. It sits on an all but abandoned block of Main Street that is now shadowed by a highway overpass. In the 1950s, Taylor Cafe was a rough-and-tumble honky-tonk that catered to itinerant agricultural workers and cotton pickers. There was a fight almost every night, remembers owner Vencil Mares. The cotton pickers are gone now and there aren't so many fights anymore, but otherwise the Taylor Cafe hasn't changed an iota in fifty years. It is a place where grizzled farmers and oil-field hands bring their grandchildren to see what barbecue joints used to look like.

White business cards hung on the wall at Louie Mueller Barbecue slowly turn deeper and deeper shades of brown.

Elgin

Named the Sausage Capital of Texas by the 1995 Texas Legislature, this little farm town is serious about sausage. Elgin sausage originated at Southside Market, whose original location in downtown Elgin opened in 1882.

Southside Market owner Ernest Bracewell Sr., a former Armour meat salesman, bought the business in 1968. Because U.S. law makes it difficult for a company to trademark a name that includes a geographic, Southside Market was unable to protect the name Elgin sausage. As a result, dozens of different companies have sprung up over the years in Elgin, each selling its own version of Elgin sausage.

Southside Market is still the leading producer, with an output of around a million pounds a year. Its logo shows the state of Texas outlined in sausage. If you stretched out a million pounds of sausage, it would actually be enough to accomplish this feat, I'm told.

In the summer, when barbecue season is in full swing, Bryan Bracewell, a grandson of the owner and chief of sausage production, guesses that all together the sausage makers in the town of Elgin turn out around a hundred thousand pounds of sausage a week. "That would be a conservative estimate," says Bryan.

Meyer's Elgin Smokehouse

188 HIGHWAY 290

512-281-3331

Meyer's Elgin Sausage is a familiar name to Central Texas barbecue fans. The sausage has been available in area grocery stores for many years. While Southside's Elgin hot sausage is all beef, Meyer's Elgin sausage comes in

Rick Schmidt at Kreuz Market.

several different varieties. The restaurant serves the all-beef and garlic pork flavors, as well as brisket, turkey, and other smoked meats. You can also have Meyer's Elgin sausage shipped to your door (see Online and Mail-Order Sources on page 288).

Old Coupland Inn

101 HOXIE STREET, COUPLAND
512-856-2777

This is a fascinating, if erratic, barbecue joint halfway between Taylor and Elgin, in the farmland east of Austin, so I have tucked it in under the Elgin listing. Coupland Tavern was founded in 1910 and featured a one-hundred-year-old back bar from the Palace Saloon in Schulenburg. Renamed

the Old Coupland Inn, it became a popular local restaurant in the 1970s and 1980s. In 1992, the building was reopened as a barbecue restaurant and dance hall. It was then sold several times, but after a string of failures, it is now under operation by the folks who revived it in 1992. Go for the barbecue, stay for the dance.

Southside Market & BBQ

1212 HIGHWAY 290 E
512-281-4650

Founded by an itinerant butcher who sold meat door to door, Southside Market is the birthplace of the legendary "Elgin hot guts," a fiery hot all-beef sausage with natural casing.

After more than a century in the old butcher shop at 109 Central Street in Elgin, the owners were unable to get fire insurance on the building. The Bracewell family moved the business out to a building on Highway 290 in 1996. The new location combines a barbecue restaurant with one of the largest sausage-making operations in the state. Southside sells its Elgin sausage both cooked and uncooked at its meat market and also from its website (see Online and Mail-Order Sources on page 288).

Six Wait-in-Line Joints

YOU USED TO HAVE TO WAIT IN LINE IF YOU WANTED BARBECUE THAT WAS hot off the smoker. And when the fresh-cooked meat was all gone, the pitmaster put the Sold Out sign on the door and went fishing. That's the way it was a hundred years ago, and that's the way it is today at a handful of the state's most talked-about new barbecue joints.

The prices are higher because they are cooking USDA Prime briskets. The meat is sliced to include buttery rendered fat and a crusty bark. The sides are heritage home-cooked cuisine, rather than the usual mass-produced potato salad and slaw from a plastic bucket.

So, is this kind of barbecue worth standing in line for? That's the subject of a heated debate these days—and a question you will have to decide for yourself.

CorkScrew BBQ

24930 BUDDE ROAD, SPRING
832-592-1184

CorkScrew BBQ is a trailer in a vacant lot beside a Woodlands area shopping center. The moist and tender USDA Prime brisket kept selling out early every day, to the chagrin of those standing in line. After turning away too many customers, owners Will and Nichole Buckman swapped out their 600-pound-capacity Cadillac steel smoker for an 1800-pound capacity J.R. Oyler rotisserie that should make a lot more people happy. Try the exceptional mac 'n' cheese, smoked tallow beans, and the Pancho and Lefty sandwich (an homage to the Willie Nelson and Merle Haggard album *Pancho & Lefty*). The sandwich features fresh-sliced brisket on a bun with the unlikely but delicious combo of *pico de gallo* and mayonnaise.

Franklin Barbecue

900 E 11TH STREET, AUSTIN
512-653-1187

Celebrity pitmaster Aaron Franklin started selling his succulent brisket from a trailer on the I-35 access road in 2009. Franklin Barbecue is now located on historic East 11th Street in the former home of Ben's Long Branch BBQ. The line that forms in front of the door in advance of Franklin's 11:00 A.M. opening guarantees a sellout every day of the week. The Tipsy Texan, a chopped brisket and purple coleslaw sandwich, is a favorite. Andrew Knowlton at *Bon Appétit* declared Franklin Barbecue the best barbecue joint in the country.

Killen's Barbecue

3613 E BROADWAY STREET, PEARLAND
281-485-2272

Killen's is a smart-looking barbecue joint in a refurbished school building. The lines are long on Saturday but not too bad on weekdays—sellout is usually around 3:00 P.M. Ronnie Killen smokes USDA Prime briskets with a rub that contains three different grinds of black pepper—coarse, medium, and fine. The result is black, crunchy bark attached to buttery rendered fat. Along with the world-class brisket, get the beef ribs and house-made sausage and don't miss the made-from-scratch creamed corn, smoked beans, and crunchy coleslaw. Desserts include bread pudding, buttermilk and pecan pies, and peach cobbler.

Rain or shine, there's always a line at Franklin Barbecue in Austin

La Barbecue
The Good Life Food Park

90 E CESAR CHAVEZ, AUSTIN

512-605-9696

Former Franklin Barbecue employee John Lewis runs the trailer officially known as La Barbecue Cuisine Texicana in an East Austin food park. The crowd lines up for brisket and pulled pork, both of which you can get in El Sancho Loco, a sandwich of pulled pork, chopped brisket, sausage, and pickled red onions. On Saturday and Sunday there's live music in the picnic grove. If it's too hot to sit around outside, get a seven-pound vacuum-sealed cooked whole brisket to go.

Pecan Lodge

2702 MAIN STREET, DALLAS

214-748-8900

Pitmaster Justin Fourton keeps the steel pits smoking and loaded with brisket, beef ribs, pork butts, and house-made sausage twenty-four hours a day at this urban hipster barbecue joint in Deep Ellum. Diane "Boss Lady" Fourton rounds out the menu with old-school Southern fried chicken, mac 'n' cheese, collard greens, and Aunt Polly's banana pudding.

The bar features microbrewery beers on draft. The line winds around the dining room and out the front door, but it's worth the wait. Bring a gang and go for The Trough, a sampler platter of every meat in the house.

Snow's BBQ

516 MAIN STREET, LEXINGTON

979-773-4640

Snow's in Lexington is about an hour east of Austin and an hour west of College Station. It's only open one day a week, on Saturday, and you need to be there very early in the morning if you hope to get any of the famous brisket and juicy pork, all of which is cooked cowboy-style over burned-down oak coals. Once a little-known secret, the place has been swamped with barbecue fanatics every Saturday since being ranked the number-one barbecue joint in the state by *Texas Monthly* magazine in 2008.

Ten Old Meat Markets and Grocery Stores

IF YOU'RE GOING TO TAKE A TREK OUT TO THE OLD MEAT MARKETS, remember that people eat lunch early in farm country. Consider skipping breakfast and showing up at 11:00 a.m. to get first choice of the day's best cuts. By 12:30 P.M., any small-town barbecue joint worth its salt has sold out of its most popular items, and these places aren't open for dinner.

Austin's BBQ & Catering

507 E MAIN STREET, EAGLE LAKE
979-234-5250

The former filling station has no charm; it's just the barbecue outlet for the old Austin's Grocery Store next door, which was established in 1950. The house sausage is outstanding—you can buy some next door to cook at home—and the brisket is usually pretty good, too. Get a couple of pounds to go and skip the tomato-heavy barbecue sauce.

City Market (Luling)

633 E DAVIS STREET,
NEAR HIGHWAY 183, LULING
830-875-9019

"We don't have any forks," the cashier at City Market repeats emphatically every five minutes. Visitors who aren't familiar with Central Texas barbecue traditions are dumbfounded by the lack of eating utensils. Why do we eat barbecue with our hands? Because that's the way cotton pickers did it, that's the way the oil-field workers did it, and that's the way it's done.

Open since 1930, Luling's City Market is an old meat market that hasn't changed much since the Depression. Try the juicy brisket and the sausage; two kinds are available, wet and dry. The wet one squirts when you cut it.

City Market (Shulenburg)

109 KESSLER AVENUE (HIGHWAY 77),
3 MILES NORTH OF SHULENBURG
979-743-3440

The "best little meat market in Texas" makes some outrageous jalapeño sausage. Quite a bit of it goes to the Salt Lick Steak House restaurant chain, but you can buy some too, if you get here early. The smoked pork loin is very popular around Christmastime. You slice it up and eat it cold. Don't forget to buy some dry sausage to eat in the car.

City Meat Market (Giddings)

101 W AUSTIN STREET, GIDDINGS
979-542-2740

There's always some brisket and sausage for lunch at City Meat Market in Giddings, but get there early because owner and pitmaster Gerald Birkelbach doesn't cook all day. This is another meat market that sidelines in barbecue. They do custom butchering too, in case you want a special cut. It's a great place to get your deer processed.

Dozier's Grocery and Market

8222 FM 359, FULSHEAR
281-346-1411

Established in 1957, Dozier's is the closest meat-market barbecue joint to downtown Houston. (It's twenty-eight miles from 610 West to Fulshear.) George H. W. Bush used to fly Dozier's pecan-smoked bacon to Washington on Air Force One.

Gonzales Food Market

311 ST. LAWRENCE STREET, GONZALES
830-672-3156

The Lopez family has been selling barbecue out of their grocery store in downtown Gonzales since 1959. The brisket is melt-in-your-mouth tender and the Tex-Mex sides are excellent.

Richard Lopez is the third-generation proprietor of Gonzales Food Market in Gonzales.

Novosad's BBQ and Sausage Market

105 S LA GRANGE STREET, HALLETTSVILLE
361-798-2770

Unusual cuts like lamb ribs and pork steaks are popular here. Try the house-made beans, coleslaw, cucumber salad, fresh-baked bread, and other pleasant (though nontraditional) twists on the old meat-market menu.

Prause Meat Market

253 W TRAVIS STREET
(HIGHWAY 71), LA GRANGE
979-968-3259

Prause's may not have the best smoked meat in the state, but it's a great place to see how the Texas barbecue joint evolved. The same family has run the market for more than a hundred years, and it's been in its present location since 1952. It's still more of a meat market than a barbecue joint—like a butcher shop with a lunch room.

Smolik's Smokehouse

501 E SAN PATRICIO AVE, MATHIS
361-547-5494

Gail Smolik and her husband Mike opened this smokehouse in 1989. It is one of two remaining outposts of a famous smoke-house chain founded by a family of Czech sausage makers. The original Smolik's Market Bar-B-Q was opened in Karnes City by William Haris Smolik in 1928. The other remaining location, Smolik's Meats & BBQ in Cuero, was founded by the late William Benedict "Bill" Smolik and is now run by Bill's son David and daughter-in-law Camille (see page 104). The Smolik family's fabulous beef and pork sausage is packed in natural casings and smoked. The recipe includes lots of garlic and black pepper. When you order, skip the brisket and get some extra sausage.

Virgie's Bar-B-Que

5535 N GESSNER DRIVE, HOUSTON
713-466-6525

Adrian Handsborough turned his family's old convenience store in the Carverdale neighborhood west of Houston, Virgie's Place, into Virgie's Bar-B-Que (Virgie is Handsborough's mother's name). The oak-smoked East Texas brisket and tender spareribs are excellent. The iced tea is sweet and so is the barbecue sauce.

Ten in the City

HATS OFF TO DANIEL VAUGHN AND HIS *PROPHETS OF SMOKED MEAT* guidebook to Texas barbecue joints. Daniel, who is now the barbecue editor of *Texas Monthly*, has visited more barbecue joints than anyone I know. His negative reviews have saved us all a lot of wasted time, and his positive reviews have made us aware of lots of barbecue joints we would have missed.

My list of barbecue joints is far more complete thanks to Daniel, even if I don't put much stock in ratings, rankings, or stars. I am also a little more sentimental than he is. I tend to forgive average barbecue in charming barbecue joints with lots of history.

The biggest problem that Daniel and I both face is that our lists go out of date as soon as they are published. Barbecue joints open and close, ownership changes, and new generations take over the pits.

So here are a few big city places I like—assuming the doors are still open.

Angelo's Bar-B-Que

2533 WHITE SETTLEMENT ROAD,
FORT WORTH
817-332-0357

The stuffed black bear that greets you at the door sets the tone. Decorated with moose heads and fishing trophies, Angelo's looks like a big, dark hunting lodge. Angelo's brisket is among the best in the state. It is smoky, perfectly seasoned, and so tender you could cut it with a pickle spear. But it's Angelo's cold draft beer that people in Fort Worth talk about. The beer schooners at Angelo's are made of thick glass and are kept in a huge freezer. When the beer is first poured into one of the glasses, it freezes along the sides.

Brooks' Place

18020 FM 529,
CYPRESS
832-893-1682

There is a picnic table chained to a trailer in the parking lot in front of Ace Hardware in suburban Cypress, northwest of Houston. That's the extent of the dining room at Brooks' Place, where pitmaster Trent Brooks turns out some of the most remarkable barbecue in East Texas. Brooks is a second-generation barbecue man; he learned from his dad, who runs a barbecue catering operation in Acres Homes. His lightly trimmed brisket has a deep smoky flavor and a crusty bark. There are also ribs, links, pulled pork, and phenomenal home-made garlic potatoes.

Gatlin's BBQ

3510 ELLA BOULEVARD,
HOUSTON
713-869-4227

The brisket is consistent, the spareribs are some of the best in the state, and the pulled pork with vinegar barbecue sauce is pushing the envelope of Texas barbecue tradition. So are the dirty rice and Creole-inflected sides and desserts. Pitmaster Greg Gatlin played defensive back for the Rice Owls football team. After graduating with degrees in economics and sports manage-ment, he got a corporate job. But the self-taught pitmaster left it all behind because he wanted to barbecue for a living. He and his mom and dad opened the original Gatlin's BBQ location in 2010.

Goode Company Barbeque

5109 KIRBY DRIVE, HOUSTON

713-522-2530

Jim Goode was a chuck-wagon cook-off competitor and barbecue buff who decided to go into business. His original restaurant on Kirby is one of the best of the new breed of Texas barbecue joints. The brisket, pork roast, and ribs are excellent. There are two choices of sausage: jalapeño and Czech.

Jackson Street BBQ

209 JACKSON STREET, HOUSTON

713-224-2400

Located next to Minute Maid Park, home of the Houston Astros, Jackson Street BBQ is the favored barbecue joint for downtown office workers and baseball fans. The co-owners both come fom Louisiana families. Greg Gatlin (see page 144) is the pitmaster, and as you might expect, his brisket and ribs are first-rate. Culinary Institute of America grad Bryan Caswell came up with the sides and the spectacular cheddar jalepeño biscuit—try a brisket burnt ends sandwich on this biscuit. Meats by the pound include smoked chicken, turkey, and two kinds of sausage as well as some excellent pulled pork. Smoked deviled eggs, dirty rice, collard greens, and meaty beans round out the side dish menu.

Patillo's Bar-B-Q

2775 WASHINGTON BOULEVARD, BEAUMONT

409-833-3156

This century-old Beaumont barbecue business is run by Frank Patillo IV. Over the years, the restaurant has been located at various Beaumont addresses. The giant pit was installed at the Washington Boulevard site in the 1950s. Look for the neon chicken sign. Patillo's serves the best version of the disappearing African-American–East Texas specialty called "juicy links" that you are likely to find. Properly served with white bread, a juicy link should ooze spicy ground beef and orange-colored melted beef fat when you cut it open. To eat it, you dab it up with the bread.

Pizzitola's Bar-B-Cue

1703 SHEPHERD DRIVE, HOUSTON

713-227-2283

When Jerry Pizzitola heard that one of his favorite barbecue joints, the old Shepherd Drive Bar-B-Q, was slated to close, he took it over and reopened it as Pizzitola's. Through an arrangement with John and Leila Davis, family members of the original owners, he was able to grandfather the brick pits that produce some of the best pork ribs in the state. Pizzitola's may be the only barbecue joint serving 2½ and down spareribs every day of the week.

Railhead Smokehouse

2900 MONTGOMERY STREET, FORT WORTH

817-738-9808

Railhead will be the first to admit that they learned everything they know from Angelo's. Like Angelo's, the Railhead has excellent brisket and tender ribs, but the population of Fort Worth seems to be divided on the subject of which establishment has colder beer. Traditionalists favor the dark interior of Angelo's, while the younger set gravitates toward the picnic tables outside at the Railhead. The next time you find yourself in Fort Worth, I suggest you try them both.

Sam's BBQ

2000 E 12TH STREET, AUSTIN

512-478-0378

This old wooden house still has a rusty screen door and an outhouse behind the woodpile. Sam's was a favorite of the late Stevie Ray Vaughan and many other blues musicians. It is still very popular with the out-all-night crowd—it's open very late. Try the ribs and the sausage. This may be the only place you'll ever find barbecued mutton (see the recipe on page 140).

Stubb's Bar-B-Q

801 RED RIVER STREET, AUSTIN

512-430-8341

The late C. B. Stubblefield was a legend in Lubbock. He not only fed up-and-coming musicians like Terry Allen and Joe Ely, but he also showed up at their sets and jammed with them. Stubb's Bar-B-Q in Austin is a music venue, bar, and restaurant. The ribs and chicken here are amazing, but the brisket is hit or miss. The Sunday Barbecue and Gospel Music Brunch is absolutely fabulous.

And Ten for the Road

LIKE MOST TEXAS FOOD LOVERS, I PLAN MY CAR TRIPS AROUND THE opening and closing times of interesting barbecue spots. These are a few of my favorite "road trip" stopovers.

Clark's Outpost

101 HIGHWAY 377, TIOGA
940-437-2414

People used to drive for hours to eat the famous barbecue at Clark's Outpost in the tiny town of Tioga, north of Denton. The place is not what it used to be, but the pork ribs are still good and so is the ham. The side dishes and desserts are the main attractions these days. There are green salads, baked potatoes, french fries, and corn on the cob, among many other vegetables. An appealing array of elaborate desserts is also offered, including bread pudding, Dutch apple pie, and a chocolate meringue pie that's over a foot tall.

Cooper's Old Time Pit Bar-B-Q

604 W YOUNG STREET
(HIGHWAY 29), LLANO
325-247-5713

No Hill Country tour is complete without a stop at Cooper's in Llano, George W. Bush's favorite barbecue joint. The meat is cooked cowboy-style over mesquite coals, and you order it straight from the pit and then take it inside to pay for it. The sirloin steak and pork chops are awesome, if you get them at

the perfect time (see Lorenzo Vences's Sirloin on page 170). The brisket is also excellent. The barbecue sauce here is bolstered with brisket juices and is truly outstanding.

Leon's "World's Finest" In & Out B-B-Q House

5427 BROADWAY AT 55TH, GALVESTON
409-744-0070

This is a good place to grab some ribs to go for lunch on the beach, but if you want to sample some awesome sides (see Leon O'Neal's Turnip Greens on page 154 and Leon's Stepped-Up Rice on page 153), sit down at one of the eight tables. The potato salad is the best you'll ever have at a barbecue joint.

Lum's Bar-B-Que

2031 N MAIN STREET, JUNCTION
325-446-3541

On the way out to Big Bend, I usually stop in Junction for a rib plate or a brisket sandwich at Lum's. It's a grocery store with a few tables inside and a really lovely picnic area outside. The meats are smoked cowboy-style over mesquite. Rumor has it that smoked goat ribs have been available, but I've never seen any. There are some enticing-looking cream pies, however.

Martin's Place

3403 S COLLEGE AVENUE, BRYAN
979-822-2031

Third-generation pitmaster Steven Kapchinskie runs Martin's Place, which is named after his grandfather, Martin Kapchinskie, who opened the business in 1924. The barbecue joint was owned by Steven's father, Albin Kapchinskie, until his death in 1980. The restaurant is frozen in time because, as Steven explains, "if I change anything, I have to get a building permit, and then I'd have to redo everything to code. Even if I just bought a new stove, I'd have to get a vent hood." Ask for a tour of the ancient pits.

Neely's Sandwich Shop

1404 E GRAND AVENUE, MARSHALL
903-935-9040

The Brown Pig, made with chopped barbecued pork on a bun with mayo and shredded lettuce, is the signature sandwich at Neely's Sandwich Shop, and it's become so iconic that most people mistakenly call the restaurant Neely's Brown Pig. When the place was founded in 1927 as Neely and Sons, the chopped pork sandwiches sold for just fifteen cents each. Hickory is burned in the restaurant's steel barbecue pit, so the pork butts, briskets, and hams are all wood-smoked. Bill Moyers, a Marshall native and Neely's fan, called it "the best sandwich between here and China."

New Zion Missionary Baptist Church Barbecue

2601 MONTGOMERY ROAD, HUNTSVILLE

936-294-0884

This combination Baptist church and barbecue joint has been called the Church of the Holy Smoke. You sit down and eat family-style at community tables in a little church hall. A Southern Pride stainless-steel oven has replaced the old-fashioned steel pits, but the tender East Texas–style ribs and brisket are still passable. Above all, save room for the wonderful homemade sides and desserts (see Huntsville Butter Beans on page 155 and Mashed Potato Salad on page 149).

The Salt Lick

18300 FM 1826, DRIFTWOOD

512-858-4959

When I was a student at the University of Texas, the Salt Lick had an all-you-can-eat family-style special for six or more people. These days my friends are more interested in the fabulous garden walk and idyllic country setting than in seeing how many ribs they can eat, but going out to the Salt Lick is still one of my favorite Sunday drives.

Steven Kapchinskie at the domino table.

Vera's Backyard Bar-B-Que

2404 SOUTHMOST ROAD, BROWNSVILLE

956-546-4159

Lovingly described by Lolis Eric Elie in his book *Smokestack Lightning*, Vera's is the last of the old-school barbacoa joints that cook foil-wrapped cows' heads in a *pozo* (pit) over mesquite and ebony coals. The best time to go to Vera's is at 8:00 or 9:00 A.M.—the heads slow-cook on the pit overnight—as the fresh, hot barbacoa meat is shredded first thing in the morning.

Zimmerhanzel's BBQ

307 ROYSTON STREET (HIGHWAY 95), SMITHVILLE

512-237-4244

Dee Dee Bunte's maiden name is Zimmerhanzel, and her family owned the building in which she and her husband, Bert Bunte,

first opened this barbecue joint about three decades ago in the charming old railroad town of Smithville. The couple tried to retire some years ago, but the townsfolk just wouldn't leave them alone. You might say that Zimmerhanzel's was coaxed back to life by popular demand. You'll see why when you sample this joint's assortment of crusty ribs, tender brisket, and coarse-ground Czech sausage with natural casings.

Community Barbecue Calendar

Five German Dance Hall Barbecues

PETERS MOTHER'S DAY BBQ
Mother's Day
Peters-Hacienda Community Hall
756 Trenckmann Road, Sealy
BBQ 11:30 A.M.
beef and pork
Cakewalk, live auction, beanbag
tournament
INFORMATION: 281-898-1346

CAT SPRINGS DANCE HALL BBQ
First Saturday in June
Cat Springs Agricultural
Society Hall
13035 Hall Road, Cat Springs
BBQ 11:00 A.M.
beef, pork, and mutton
The oldest community barbecue
in Texas, dating back 150 years
INFORMATION: 979-865-2540

MILLHEIM HARMONIE VEREIN'S ANNUAL FATHER'S DAY BARBECUE
Father's Day
Millheim Harmonie Verein's
Dance Hall
3384 FM 949 Road (15 miles
east of Cat Springs), Sealy
BBQ 11:00 A.M.
beef, mutton, and pork
Cake wheel, silent auction,
music; one of the last of the
old-fashioned open pits
INFORMATION: 979-877-4408

KENNEY 4TH OF JULY BBQ
July 4
Kenney Agricultural Society Hall
(off highway 36 north of Bellville),
Kenney
BBQ 11:00 A.M.
beef, mutton, and pork
Cake wheel, silent auction, live
music; barbecue is more than a
century old
INFORMATION: 979-865-0329
(KENNEY POST OFFICE)

SONS OF HERMANN WASHINGTON LODGE BBQ
Third Sunday in October
Sons of Hermann Lodge
9499 FM 1370, Washington
BBQ 11:00 A.M.
brisket and pork butt, homemade-
desserts table
Cake auction, raffle

Three Big Barbecues

DUMAS DOGIE DAYS
Wednesday through Sunday of
the second weekend in June
McDade Park, Dumas
BBQ 11:00 A.M.
The town celebration that began
as the Dumas Annual Old Settler's
Reunion and Rodeo became
Dumas Dogie Days in 1946. The
Dumas Lions Club donates the
proceeds to local charities. An
average of 7,600 pounds of meat
are cooked in a covered pit with
15 cords of wood for 24 hours
and served with 40 gallons of
barbecue sauce, 800 pounds of
beans, 200 pounds of onions,
228 gallon cans of peaches, and
300 loaves of bread to between
5,000 and 6,000 people.

XIT RODEO AND REUNION
First long weekend (Thursday to
Sunday) in August
Dalhart
Free beef barbecue on Saturday;
other free barbecue each night.
Some 10,000 pounds of beef are
cooked each year in an under-
ground pit for "the world's largest
free barbecue." The event began
in 1936, when cowboys and their
families who worked on the now-
defunct XIT Ranch began to get
together for an annual reunion to
reminisce about life on the ranch.

Mutton ribs are an old-fashioned favorite you can still find at community barbecues.

Since 1937, these reunions have been held in Dalhart with a parade and barbecue for the public. In recent years, the event has been expanded to include a free feed every night; in 2014, barbecued chicken wings on Thursday and barbecued pork chops on Friday, leading up to the main barbecue event on Saturday.

ST. LOUIS DAY
CELEBRATION BBQ
Sunday closest to August 25
(Feast of St. Louis)
St. Louis Catholic Church
610 Madrid Street, Castroville
830-931-2826
According to Daniel Vaughn, in 2014, some 6,000 pounds of sausage and brisket were barbecued at the annual St. Louis Day Celebration in Castroville, which has been held on the weekend closest to the Feast of St. Louis for over 130 years. St. Louis Catholic Church in Castroville was founded in 1870, and a Texas historical marker near the statue of St. Louis at the front of the church mentions the St. Louis Day tradition. It reads, "Men smoked sausage and pit barbecued beef. Women prepared potato salad, cabbage slaw, and desserts."

Whole calves were cooked in open pits at the early St. Louis celebrations, but by the 1960s, briskets had been substituted. In the 1990s, enclosed steel cookers replaced the old open pits.

A BARBECUE GLOSSARY

Barbacoa

Just as the word *barbecue* has many meanings in English, the word *barbacoa* has many meanings in Spanish. In Mexico City, barbacoa is lamb or goat meat wrapped in maguey leaves and roasted on hot coals. In Texas, Mexican ranch hands adapted this interior Mexican style of barbacoa to roast cows' heads, or *cabezas*. They wrapped them in maguey leaves, and later in aluminum foil and canvas, and buried them in earthen pits with hot coals. In the Tejano tradition, the term *barbacoa* has come to mean the meat from the head of a steer, whether it is prepared in a smoker or steamed in a conventional oven.

Beans

Whether you're cooking dried pinto beans, butter (lima) beans, or any other variety, you have probably heard a lot of different opinions on how it should be done. Some people recommend that, to aid digestibility, you soak beans overnight and change the water. Most Mexican cooks insist that adding salt to beans before they're done makes them tough. How much truth is there to any of this?

In an article in the *Los Angeles Times*, food editor Russ Parsons challenged these old nuggets of wisdom. According to Parsons, his own independent testing revealed that soaking the beans didn't aid digestibility, but it did hurt the flavor and texture. He also said that salting the water while the beans were cooking had no effect on tenderness but did improve the taste.

According to the bean scientists at the California Dried Bean Advisory Board, acids such as those present in tomatoes, chiles, and vinegar will slow the tenderizing process, so these ingredients should be added after the beans are cooked.

Black Pepper

Almost every barbecue rub calls for black pepper. Some cook-off competitors swear by whole Malabar black peppercorns, freshly ground or cracked. Others favor peppercorns from Tellicherry and Lampong. Some pitmasters combine finely ground black pepper and coarse ground black pepper in the same rub.

Using cracked pepper in a rub gives the meat a distinctive flavor. Cracked pepper is very different from freshly ground pepper. The aroma and flavor of the peppercorn comes through in every bite. To make cracked pepper, you need to crush each peppercorn into no more than eight or ten pieces. You can put whole peppercorns in a large frying pan and use a smaller frying pan to crush them, but you really need to bear down hard, and this takes a lot of strength.

The easiest cracking method is to put the peppercorns in a food processor or spice grinder and pulse it once or twice. This method takes patience and usually requires several batches. You have to sort through the cracked peppercorns, remove the remaining whole peppercorns, and repeat the process. The simplest way to keep cracked peppercorns is to buy a bottle of whole black peppercorns, crack them all, and then return them to the same bottle for storage.

Chickens

The recipes in this book were tested with unenhanced (not potassium- or salt-water-injected) supermarket fryers. You can substitute free-range chickens or roasting hens if you want, but remember that the larger birds require longer cooking times. Since the skin on a barbecued chicken tends to get too dark anyway, you may want to wrap a larger chicken in aluminum foil when it reaches the desired color.

Chiles

We often use the words *chile* and *pepper* interchangeably in the Southwest, but we often use them together, too. One reason for the popularity of the redundant term *chile pepper* is that the words *chili* and *chile* refer to specific dishes in Texas and New Mexico. *Chili* means "chili con carne," but it is actually an alternate spelling of *chile* and is pronounced the same in English.

FRESH CHILES Fresh chiles are usually harvested in the green stage. Fully ripened red chiles are most often used for drying, but they also sometimes turn up fresh in the supermarket. Green or red chiles can be used interchangeably unless the recipe specifies the color. The following fresh chiles, listed from mildest to hottest, appear in this book.

Jalapeño Hot, green, and bullet shaped, the jalapeño is the classic Tex-Mex hot pepper and one of the world's best-known chiles. Originally grown in Mexico, it is named for Jalapa, a town in the state of Veracruz. The fresh jalapeño has a strong, vegetal flavor to go with the heat. I prefer to cook with fresh jalapeños, but the jalapeño is most widely consumed in its pickled form in Texas. Along with barbecue sauce, pickles, and raw onions, pickled jalapeños are a popular condiment in Texas barbecue joints.

Serrano Similar to the jalapeño, the serrano is hotter and smaller. Most Mexicans claim that serranos have a fuller, more herbaceous flavor. Since the vast majority of jalapeños are pickled, the serrano is actually the most widely used fresh chile in Texas.

Pequín Also known as piquin, chili-piquin, or chiltepin, this tiny chile grows wild throughout southern Texas and northern Mexico. Although "pequín" seems to be a corruption of the Spanish *pequeño*, meaning "small," the Spanish name itself is probably a corruption of *chiltecpin*, a Nahuatl word meaning flea chile, a reference to both the size and sting of the chile. Since these chiles were spread by birds rather than cultivation, experts tell us that pequíns are the oldest chiles in North America. In northern Mexico, they are collected in the wild and sold in markets, where they fetch more than almost any other kind of chile. They are sometimes dried and preserved for year-round use. A pequín bush can be found in almost any backyard or vacant lot in South Texas, which means that pequíns are common in home cooking. Because they are not grown commercially, they are seldom found in restaurant cooking or in grocery stores. If you find some, you can substitute three or four fresh pequíns for one serrano or half a jalapeño.

Handling Chiles

It's wise to wear rubber gloves when handling jalapeños and serranos. Get a little juice from the cut-up pepper on your face or in your eyes and you can count on 10 minutes of sheer agony. If you don't have rubber gloves, use a piece of plastic wrap to hold the chile while you cut it. Clean the knife and the cutting board immediately with hot soapy water. If your hands are exposed to the volatile juice, try soaking them for a few minutes in a mild bleach solution.

Roasting Fresh Chiles

To roast a fresh chile, place it whole over a high flame on a barbecue grill or on a gas stove and turn it as needed to blister the skin on all sides. Don't allow the flame to burn too long in one place, or you'll burn through it. After most of the skin is well blistered, wrap the warm chile in a wet paper towel and set it aside to steam gently. When you remove the towel, most of the skin should come off with it. Scrape off the rest of the skin with a butter knife.

DRIED CHILES The following dried chiles are used in recipes in this book.

Ancho The dried form of the poblano chile, the ancho is very dark brown and wide (the word *ancho* means "wide" in Spanish). Anchos are the fleshiest of the dried chiles, and their pulp combines a little bitterness with a sweetness reminiscent of raisins. They are usually mild, although occasionally one will surprise you with its heat.

Chipotle The chipotle is a smoke-dried jalapeño. Small, wrinkled, and light brown, chipotles have an incredibly rich, smoky flavor and are usually very hot. Smoking as a method of preserving jalapeños was already common in Mexico when the Spanish first arrived. The original Nahuatl spelling, *chilpotle*, is also sometimes seen.

To make chipotle chile powder, you need to use dried chipotles, but canned chipotles are acceptable in sauce recipes. Because canned chipotles are prepared in some kind of sauce, usually a vinegary adobo sauce, there is no need to soak them as described in Soaking and Puréeing Dried Chiles (below). Instead, just stem and seed them as directed and purée them with some of the sauce from the can.

Guajillo Tapered and with smooth, shiny reddish skin, the guajillo has a tart, medium-hot flavor. Dried Anaheims are also sometimes called guajillos, but Anaheims are much milder than the true guajillo. The guajillo makes a pleasantly sweet-hot chile powder and can be substituted for, or added to, ancho chiles in barbecue sauce.

Pasilla Long and skinny, the pasilla has black, slightly wrinkled skin and a strong, satisfying bitter flavor, and it can range from medium-hot to hot. The name comes from the Spanish *pasa*, meaning "raisin," a reference to the appearance of the skin. The pasilla is commonly ground for chile powder and can also be used in place of, or added to, ancho chiles in barbecue sauce.

Soaking and Puréeing Dried Chiles
There's not much to it. Just put the dried chiles in a bowl with enough hot water to cover them. Put a saucer or an upside-down coffee mug on top of the chiles to keep them submerged and leave them until they are soft. This usually takes 15 to 30 minutes. Chipotles are typically very hard and tend to take

longer. You can speed up the process by simmering them gently in water on the stove top.

If you're making a chile purée for a barbecue sauce, you want the chiles very soft, so you'll need to leave them in the water longer. When they are soft enough, pull the stems off and scoop out the seeds. Put the flesh in the blender with enough of the soaking water to get the blades turning and purée until smooth. Because chiles vary in size, you'll have to estimate how much purée you'll get. Anchos yield the most purée; guajillos and other shiny-skinned, less fleshy varieties yield very little. When selecting chiles to make a purée, use the softest, most pliable ones available.

You can boost the flavor of the purée a little by soaking the chiles in hot stock instead of hot water. If you're making a sauce for brisket, use beef stock. Chicken stock is good for chicken or pork.

Chili Powder and Chile Powder

Several of the recipes in this book call for chili powder, while others call for chile powder. These are two different things. Chili powder, which is sold in most grocery stores, contains ground chile peppers along with cumin and other spices and/or herbs. It was invented by the Gebhardt Company in San Antonio in the late 1800s.

Chile powder is made of pure ground chile peppers. For example, paprika, which can be sweet, medium-hot, or hot, is a chile powder. You can buy other chile powders at some gourmet or ethnic stores, or you can make them at home in an electric coffee grinder. Making your own chile powders allows you to use such flavorful peppers as chipotles, guajillos, and pasillas in your cooking. Select brittle dried peppers for this purpose, or put pliant dried peppers into a 350°F oven for 10 minutes to dry them out.

Clean all of the coffee out of the grinder. (You may want to grind a little salt or cornmeal to rid the grinder of any coffee residue.) Stem and seed the chile and cut it into pieces small enough to fit easily into the grinder. Grind the chile for a minute or so, or until reduced to a fine powder. I keep several bottles of chile powder on my spice rack, labeled by variety.

If you decide to make chile powder at home, remember to clean the pepper out of the grinder, or you'll have some very interesting coffee the next morning.

Epazote

Prized as a pungent herb in southern Mexico, epazote is called "pigweed" by gardeners in the United States. Once seldom used in northern Mexican or Tex-Mex cooking, it is now enjoying a new popularity because it is a traditional seasoning with black beans. Although often difficult to find in grocery stores, it is, oddly enough, easy to find in your garden. It has a jagged leaf that looks something like marijuana and has a strong soapy smell vaguely reminiscent of cilantro. If you pull some up and

decide to use it in your cooking, consult an herbalist, botanist, or gardening expert to be sure you've got the right stuff. Pigweed is so common, however, that once you can identify it, you'll never have to buy it again.

Hog Casings

Because so many Texans make venison sausage, you can find medium hog casings in most Texas grocery stores during deer season. But even if you don't live in Texas, natural sausage casings aren't that hard to find. Ask your butcher, look in the yellow pages under Butcher's Supplies, or check online.

You need about ten feet of casings for five pounds of sausage, but you'll probably have to buy a lot more than that. The casings come packed in salt in fairly big plastic tubs. But don't worry if you have more than you need; they are packed in salt so they keep forever.

Hot-Pepper Sauces

Some of the recipes in this book specify Tabasco sauce as an ingredient. Others call for Louisiana hot sauce. What I mean when I say hot-pepper sauce is a solution of vinegar or other liquid in which pepper solids and flavorings are suspended. This kind of sauce comes in a shaker bottle. Chunky salsas and *picante* sauces are not the same thing.

Louisiana is famous for its pepper sauces. So is Mexico. Some are much hotter than others. For example, habanero hot-pepper sauces tend to be incendiary. You can use the pepper sauces interchangeably, thereby making your food as hot as you like it.

Mexican Oregano

Mexican oregano is a member of the verbena family and is very different from Mediterranean oregano. It can be found dried in Mexican markets and some supermarkets, but it is sometimes difficult to find fresh. Planting a little in your garden is the best guarantee of having some on hand.

MSG

If you want to be a barbecue judge, you'd better not be too sensitive to this stuff. Monosodium glutamate, a.k.a. MSG, is one reason that so many cook-off competitors like to keep their recipes secret. Because MSG has gotten such a bad name, nobody wants to admit that the barbecue rub is spiked with it. But the truth is, the stuff really does make things taste better, and if I were trying to win a barbecue cook-off, I would use it too. Barbecue joints, on the other hand, have had to stop using MSG because so many people complain about it. It's used in many commercial rubs and barbecue sauces, so check the ingredients list carefully if you want to avoid it.

Rice

Long-grain white rice will work fine, but I much prefer the long-grain basmati hybrid called Texmati. It is aromatic and retains a nutty firmness when cooked. Basmati is an excellent substitute.

Salt

Several varieties of salt are called for in this book because the folks who gave me the recipes all have their favorites. Table salt (sodium chloride) is mined salt that is mixed with additives to keep it free-flowing, and it often also includes iodine (sodium iodide) in areas where the diet is deficient in this important mineral. It tastes saltier than kosher salt or sea salt. If a recipe calls for "salt," table salt is what we're talking about.

Kosher salt is pure mined salt, and it is often used in meat curing.

Sea salt is made from sea water by a more costly evaporative process. Sea salt has become the preferred salt of many gourmets because of its flavor. It will work fine in most of the recipes in this book.

Smoked Tomatoes

While you have your barbecue going, I highly recommend that you get into the habit of smoking a few tomatoes. Smoked tomatoes are the secret of truly great sauces and salsas. Generally, you can place tomatoes on the barbecue for half an hour, but smoking times will vary. Roma tomatoes tend to take longer. Tender summer tomatoes will not take long at all. Substitute the smoked tomatoes for fresh tomatoes in salsas or any recipe that calls for tomatoes.

Tejano

The word *tejano* simply means "Texan" in modern Spanish, but it has taken on much wider connotations. Mexican-Americans of Texan ancestry also call themselves Tejanos. Some Tejano families trace their heritage back to the state's original settlers. They are the Texas equivalent of New England families whose ancestors came over on the Mayflower. As Tejanos are fond of pointing out, they didn't immigrate to the United States; the border moved south.

Tomatillos

Husk-covered tomatillos, which are tart and nearly always cooked before eating, are widely available in grocery stores. Look for firm, unblemished tomatillos with tight husks. Many Mexican cooks say that the smaller tomatillos are more flavorful.

Tortillas

Nowadays, many grocery stores stock a wide variety of tortillas. There are plain and flavored flour tortillas, fluffy white corn tortillas, and old-fashioned corn tortillas. The old-fashioned corn ones, sometimes called enchilada tortillas, are the most common. They are very thin and somewhat leathery but hold up well in cooking. Save these for frying. Use the flour tortillas and fluffy white corn tortillas for serving at the table; flour for sausage wraps and brisket tacos, corn with barbacoa and lengua.

Heating Tortillas

Store-bought flour or corn tortillas need to be heated before serving. The easiest method is to wrap them in aluminum foil and stick them in a 350°F oven for 5 to 10 minutes. Corn tortillas can also be wrapped in a clean dish towel that has been slightly dampened and put into the oven. The moisture from the towel will steam them slightly and improve their texture as they warm up.

When you need only a few flour tortillas, it's even easier to put them into an ungreased skillet over medium heat and to flip them quickly as they warm, shuffling the tortillas until each side has been in contact with the skillet for 10 seconds or so.

ONLINE AND MAIL-ORDER SOURCES

Barbecue

Lots of Texas barbecue restaurants cater major events all over the country. Just contact the restaurant of your choice. Some will also ship small amounts of heat-and-serve barbecue by overnight delivery service. Here are a few you can try.

City Market

(SCHULENBURG)

"The best little meat market in Texas" ships its famous jalapeño sausage, as well as ready-to-eat snacks like dry jerky-style sausage and peppered pork tenderloin by overnight express.
www.citymarketsch.com
800-793-3440

County Line Barbecue

(10 LOCATIONS)

The County Line is a very successful barbecue restaurant chain with locations in Austin, San Antonio, Houston, El Paso, and Albuquerque. The restaurants are very clean and attractive, and the barbecue is generally very good, too. For overnight delivery, call 800-AIR-RIBS (247-7427).
www.airribs.com

Goode Company and Barbecue

At Goode Company's online store, you can buy smoked brisket, ribs, sausage and smoked turkeys, barbecue rubs and sauces, hats and t-shirts, and a wide assortment of gift baskets including one that contains this book. But the biggest seller by far is an outstanding pecan pie packaged in a sturdy wooden box.
www.goodecompany.com

The Salt Lick

The Salt Lick in Driftwood sells barbecued meats, barbecue sauce, rubs, salsa, and t-shirts online along with their cookbook and gift certificates.
www.saltlickbbq.com

Snow's BBQ

Texas Monthly's number-one barbecue joint in 2008 ships a wide variety of meats, sauces, and souvenirs.
www.snowsbbq.com
979-542-8189

Elgin Sausage

There's nothing quite like Texas barbecue sausage, and it ships pretty well. Once you try it, you'll be back for more.

Meyer's Elgin Smokehouse

Choose from these flavors: plain, garlic, sage, beef, or hot.
800-677-6465

Southside Market

Southside can ship you its famous sausage already smoked and ready to reheat, along with its summer sausages, hot sauce, and barbecue sauce. Gift boxes are also available.
www.southsidemarket.com
512-281-4650

Dry Rubs and Sauces

Adams Rubs

Adams makes an excellent brisket rub that contains plenty of salt, pepper, and spices and the natural meat tenderizer papain, but no MSG.
www.adamsextract.com
512-359-3050

Adkins Western Style Barbecue Seasoning

A favorite North Texas blend. Gift packs of various seasoning mixes are also available.
www.adkinsbbq.com
800-356-2914

Bolner's Fiesta

This famous San Antonio spice company makes brisket rub, rib rub, pork rub, and chicken rub, along with barbecue crab seasoning, fajita seasoning, and chili mix. Buy a case and get a discount.
www.fiestaspices.com

Butt Rub

Created by Texas native and Culinary Institute of America grad Byron Chism, this is one of the most popular pork rubs in the country among cook-off competitors.
www.buttrub.com
850-267-3661

Craig's Texas Pepper Jelly

Craig Sherry, proprietor of Texas Pepper Jelly, was the Grand Champion Cook at the 2011 Houston Livestock Show and Rodeo Barbecue Cook-Off. His pepper jellies have become the winningest glazes on the barbecue circuit. Popular flavors include the following:
Apple Habanero Pepper Jelly
Cherry Habanero Pepper Jelly
Mango Habanero Rib Candy
Pineapple Habanero Pepper Jelly
www.texaspepperjelly.com
713-702-3489

Daigle's Cajun Sweet & Sour

The Daigle family's famous Cajun sweet-hot sauces have become a favorite rib and chicken glaze for barbecue competitors. Gayle Daigle at Daigle Family Co. takes orders by Internet or over the phone. "We are one call away if you would like help with a recipe," Gayle promises on the family website. Favorite products include:
Cajun Sweet & Sour Sauce
Cajun Sweet & Sour Sauce Spicy
Cajun Sweet Pecan Garlic Sauce
Cajun Sweet Applewood
    Jalapeno Sauce
Cajun Sweet Habanero Rib Sauce
www.cajunsweetandsoursauce
.com
337-298-7897

Harley's Texas Style Bar-B-Que Seasoning

The winningest cook-off competitor in Texas sells his own dry rub, with or without MSG.
www.harleysseasoning.com
866-478-1851

TexJoy Bar-B-Q Seasoning

The favorite dry rub at New Zion Missionary Baptist Church Barbecue and many other Texas barbecue joints.
www.texjoy.com
800-259-3400

Stubb's Rubs and Bar-B-Q Sauces

Although the master, C. B. Stubblefield, has passed on, his legend lives on in spice rubs and sauces worthy of their namesake.
www.stubbsbbq.com
512-480-0203

Fuel

B&B Charcoal

Lump oak charcoal and lump hardwood charcoals.
www.bbcharcoal.com
855-BBQ-COAL (227-2625)

Western Premium BBQ Products

The largest selection of woods for barbecue in Texas, including orange, peach, and other exotic fruitwoods.
www.woodinc.com
830-569-2501

Cows' Heads for Barbacoa

If your grocery store or meat market cannot get you a cow's head for barbacoa, you can call Sam Kane in Corpus Christi and arrange a shipment.
www.kanebeef.com
316-241-5000

BARBECUE ASSOCIATIONS

Texas barbecue cook-off participants keep track of upcoming events, who is winning what, changes in the rules, and general gossip through barbecue associations. Several of these groups have newsletters that they can send you for more information about barbecue cook-offs in your area.

Central Texas Barbecue Association (CTBA) WWW.CTBABBQ.COM

International Barbeque Cookers Association (IBCA) WWW.IBCABBQ.ORG

Lone Star Barbecue Society (LSBS) WWW.LONESTARBARBECUE.COM

National Barbecue Association (NBBQA) WWW.NBBQA.ORG

Texas Gulf Coast BBQ Cookers Association (TGCBCA) WWW.TGCBCA.ORG

West Texas Barbecue Association (WTBA) WWW.WTBABBQ.TRIPOD.COM

The mission of Foodways Texas is to preserve, promote and celebrate the diverse food cultures of Texas. FoodwaysTexas.com

Bibliography

Aidells, Bruce, and Denis Kelly. *The Complete Meat Cookbook*. New York: Houghton Mifflin, 1998.

Andrews, Jean. *Peppers: The Domesticated Capsicums*. Austin: University of Texas Press, 1984.

Bayless, Rick. *Authentic Mexican*. New York: Morrow, 1987.

Caro, Robert A. *The Path to Power*. New York: Vintage, 1981.

Cusik, Heidi Haughy. *Soul and Spice: African Cooking in the Americas*. San Francisco: Chronicle Books, 1995.

Dearen, Patrick. *A Cowboy of the Pecos*. Plano: Republic of Texas Press, 1997.

Dobie, J. Frank. *A Vaquero of the Brush Country*. Austin: University of Texas Press, reissue edition (originally published by Southwest Press, 1929), 1998.

Ellis, Merle. *Cutting Up in the Kitchen: A Butcher's Guide to Saving Money on Meat and Poultry*. San Francisco: Chronicle Books, 1975.

Ferber, Edna. *Giant*. New York: Doubleday, 1952.

Flemmons, Jerry. *More Texas Siftings*. Fort Worth: Texas Christian University Press, 1997.

Foley, Neil. *White Scourge: Mexicans, Blacks, and Poor Whites in Texas Cotton Culture*. Berkeley: University of California Press, 1999.

Kafka, Barbara. *Roasting*. New York: Morrow, 1995.

Linck, Ernestine Sewell, and Joyce Gibson Roach. *Eats: A Folk History of Texas Food*. Fort Worth: Texas Christian University Press, 1992.

Luchetti, Cathy. *Home on the Range: A Culinary History of the American West*. New York: Villard, 1993.

Price, Byron B. *National Cowboy Hall of Fame Chuck Wagon Cookbook*. New York: Hearst Books, 1995.

Thorne, John. *Serious Pig*. New York: North Point Press, 1996.

Online Sources

The Handbook of Texas Online: www.TSHAonline.org

Farm Security Administration / Office of War Information Transcripts: American Memory Collections, Library of Congress: Memory.loc.gov/ammem

Photo Credits

BETTMAN/CORBIS: 208–209
LBJ Library, Robert Knudsen: 167
LBJ Library, Yoichi Okamoto: 36, 132
Robert Jacob Lerma: 11, 14, 43, 46–47,
    56, 61, 73, 76, 81, 86, 88, 92–93,
    121, 126, 144, 158–159, 169, 183,
    236–237, 245, 254, 255, 264–265,
    267, 268, 269, 271, 273, 277, 279,
    294, 303
Library of Congress, FSA-OWI
    Collection, Dorothea Lange: 179
Library of Congress, FSA-OWI
    Collection, Russell Lee: 4–5,
    100–101, 136–137, 176–177
Courtesy Karen Mayberry: 146
Wyatt McSpadden: 29, 96–97, 116–117,
    216–217
Michael Murphy: 20-21
Texas State Library Archives Division:
    2–3, 22–23, 31, 32–33, 34
University of Texas, Arlington, Fort
    Worth Star Telegram Collection
The UT Institute of Texan Cultures,
    no. 84-484, Courtesy of Margaret
    Virginia Crain Lowery: 26–27
The UT Institute of Texan Cultures,
    no. 80–516, Courtesy of the Estate of
    Roger Fleming: 30
The UT Institute of Texan Cultures,
    no. 76-388, Courtesy of Mrs. Stacy
    Labaj: 122–123
The UT Institute of Texan Cultures,
    no. 96-384, Courtesy of Pat S.
    Woods: 131
The UT Institute of Texan Cultures,
    no. 3042-D, The San Antonio Light
    Collection: 230–231
The UT Institute of Texan Cultures,
    no. 3042-F, The San Antonio Light
    Collection: Cover, 161
The UT Institute of Texan Cultures,
    no. 4-26-1990 F, The San Antonio
    Express-News Collection: 193
Scott Van Osdol: 38–39
Will van Overbeek: 12–13
Robb Walsh: 51, 53, 80, 104, 139, 141,
    150–151, 170, 182, 187, 190–191, 195,
    198–199, 200–201, 228, 242, 246,
    251, 252, 287

Permissions

Acknowledgments

Thanks to Bill LeBlond at Chronicle Books for taking a chance fifteen years ago, and to D.J. Stout for a design that has stood the test of time. Thanks to Amy Treadwell, Doug Ogan, Alice Chau, and Tera Killip at Chronicle Books for bringing this second edition to life. And thanks to Dr. Jeff Savell and the gang at Texas A&M Meat Science Center for sharing their passion for Texas barbecue.

I am grateful to Marvin Bendele, Bryan Caswell, John T. Edge, Elizabeth Engelhardt, Randy Evans, Levi Goode, Jim Gossen, Chris Shepherd, Kelly Yandell, and all the other folks who pulled together to get Foodways Texas off the ground. And I invite all Texas barbecue lovers to join the organization and help us preserve and celebrate the history of Texas barbecue.

Thanks to all the pitmasters, cook-off competitors, and restaurant owners who took the time to talk to me and help me with recipes and advice, especially Robert Sierra, Ernest Servantes, Will and Nichole Buckman, Justin and Diane Fourton, Aaron Franklin, Vencil Mares, Harley Goerlitz, Marvin Lange, Tommy Wimberly, Rockney Terry, Bill Smolik, Louis Charles Henley, Bryan Bracewell, Rick Schmidt, John Fullilove, Willie Mays, and Leon O'Neal.

Thanks to the outstanding photographers who have contributed to this book, especially Robert Lerma, Will van Overbeek, Michael Murphy, Scott Van Osdol, and Wyatt McSpadden.

And thanks to my fellow Texas barbecue writers for all the inspiration, help, and goodwill, especially Daniel Vaughn, J. C. Reid, Bud Kennedy, and Jim Shahin.

Many thanks also to the Houston Livestock Show and Rodeo Barbecue Cook-Off, the Taylor International Barbecue Cook-Off, and to the entire fraternity of barbecue cook-off organizers, volunteers, judges, and competitors.

Barbecue fans owe a special debt of gratitude to the families who maintain the Lone Star State's unique traditions, especially the Mueller family, the Burney family, the Black family, the Bracewell family, the Mays family, the Smolik family, the Schmidt family, the Gatlin family, and the Goode family. Their dedication to preserving the culinary culture and folklore of Texas is an inspiration to food lovers everywhere.

Pitmaster Jason Tedford stokes the fire at Louie Mueller in Taylor.

Index